Mike Meyers'
A+ Certification
Lab Manual

Michael Meyers
Cary Dier

Osborne/**McGraw-Hill**

New York Chicago San Francisco Lisbon London
Madrid Mexico City Milan New Delhi San Juan
Seoul Singapore Sydney Toronto

Osborne/**McGraw-Hill**
2600 Tenth Street
Berkeley, California 94710
U.S.A.

To arrange bulk purchase discounts for sales promotions, premiums, or fund-raisers, please contact
Osborne/**McGraw-Hill** at the above address. For information on translations or book distributors outside the
U.S.A., please see the International Contact Information page immediately following the text of this book.

Mike Meyers' A+ Certification Lab Manual

234567890 DOC DOC 01987654321

ISBN 0-07-219126-0

Publisher
Brandon A. Nordin

Vice President & Associate Publisher
Scott Rogers

Editorial Director
Gareth Hancock

Senior Acquisitions Editor
Michael Sprague

Project Manager
Deidre Dolce

Project Editor
Laurie Stewart

Acquisitions Coordinator
Paulina Pobocha

Copy Editor
Nicole LeClerc

Proofreaders
Andrea Fox
KJ Malkovitch

Indexer
Jack Lewis

Computer Designer
Maureen Forys, Happenstance Type-O-Rama

Series Design
Maureen Forys, Happenstance Type-O-Rama

Cover Design
Patti Lee

This book was composed with QuarkXPress 4.11 on a Macintosh G4.

I'd like to raise a pint to the great folks on the A+ newsgroup (alt.certification.aplus). This one's for you!

—M.M.

This one's for Betsy Ramsey, uber-geek and best of friends, who introduced me to computers more than two decades ago.

—C.D.

Contents

About the Authors

Michael Meyers is the industry's leading authority on A+ Certification. He is president and founder of Total Seminars, LLC, a major provider of PC and network repair seminars for thousands of organizations throughout the world and member of CompTIA. Mike is the author of the best-selling *All-in-One A+ Certification Exam Guide*.

Cary Dier, as befits a Gemini, counts the disparate fields of computers and medieval history as her two primary interests. Currently, she's making a living writing and editing computer books, following a career as a lawyer for the (as the papers always put it) "super-secret" NSA, and living the life of an impoverished grad student in history for a number of years. A native Vermonter, she can't entirely believe she's living in Houston, Texas, where she serves as house-human for two spoiled feline companions, Oliver and Sophie.

Acknowledgments

Like all such projects, this was a group effort. At the top of our acknowledgments list is Roger Conrad whose efforts were critical to making this manual happen. Close behind him is Scott Jernigan, editor extraordinaire and our favorite bard. We'd also like to thank all the superior folks at Osborne/McGraw-Hill, including Michael Sprague, Paulina Pobocha, and Deidre Dolce, as well as the freelance team of Laurie Stewart, Maureen Forys, Nicole LeClerc, Andrea Fox, and KJ Malkovitch. And last but not least, here at Total Seminars, Dudley, Janelle, Amber, Cindy, Lloyd, Dana, Martin, John, and Bambi. It's great to be on their team.

Introduction

Welcome to the lab manual that accompanies your *All-In-One A+ Certification Exam Guide* (Osborne/McGraw-Hill, 2001). This lab manual provides lots of interesting hands-on activities that bring the knowledge you gained from the textbook to life. Whether you are taking an exam preparation course or learning by yourself, you'll love the challenging labs provided by this book.

In keeping with any type of hands-on course, please use extreme care when working with PCs. The electronics inside the typical PC are extremely sensitive to electrostatic discharge (ESD), and you'll want to be very careful when working inside your PC to avoid destroying some of its parts. The main textbook goes into detail about the proper anti-static procedures, but let's review a few points—and cover a few new ones—to ensure that your PC survives these labs without any damage from ESD.

Before You Begin

Use Anti-ESD Equipment

At the very least, use a good anti-ESD wristband, which is available at any electronics store. The wristband (see Figure 1) has an alligator clip that you attach to a part of your PC's frame. Most techs like to clip onto some part of the power supply vent grating, but any part of a PC's metallic frame works great.

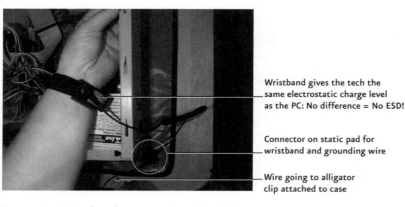

Wristband gives the tech the same electrostatic charge level as the PC: No difference = No ESD!

Connector on static pad for wristband and grounding wire

Wire going to alligator clip attached to case

Figure 1 Wristband connections detailed

An anti-static mat provides another layer of protection from ESD. The mat connects to both the PC and the wristband, making sure that you, the PC, and any equipment placed on the mat all share the same electrical potential. Figure 2 shows my editor, Scott Jernigan, using an anti-static mat and wristband while hard at work on his new "dream machine."

FIGURE 2 A static-free Scott Jernigan

You can purchase even better anti-ESD equipment than I've mentioned here, but for most of us, the wristband and mat combination will protect the PC's sensitive components from all but the worst power surges.

What if you don't have a wristband and mat? My first response is, "Get them!" But sometimes you have to fix a PC problem and you can't stop for a trip to the computer store. In that case, follow these steps to minimize the risk of ESD damage:

1. Try to avoid generating static electricity. Some common culprits of static electricity are Styrofoam cups, mini-vacs (okay for keyboards, but not for internal boards), socks on rugs, synthetic fibers, low humidity in general, and rubbing a balloon on your head.

2. Try to dissipate any static electricity you may have built up. Make it a habit to touch your PC's power supply (or if that's not possible, the case) when you approach the machine, *before* you touch any other part. This will equalize your electrical potential and the machine's. Any time you move around, touch the power supply again in case you have built up a new charge.

Unplug the Power Supply

Despite years of good techs yelling, "Don't plug in the power supply!" the old "plug it in or not" argument continues to plague us. I never put my hands inside a PC while it is plugged in—if you want to argue this tired concept, send me an email at esd@totalsem.com and we'll discuss it.

Even though the power supply stays unplugged from the household current, try to keep the motherboard power plug inserted in the motherboard while working to guarantee that the power supply and the metal frame of the PC are at the same electrical potential as the motherboard. Remember, most PCs continue to feed power to the motherboard even if they are off so be sure to unplug the power cable from the wall outlet.

Handle All Parts Correctly

Never grab any electronic component in such a way that your hands contact (and leave skin oils or dirt on) anything that could be hurt from ESD. In most cases, you just need to use a little common sense. Also, avoid direct contact with expansion slots and connectors. While the ESD risk is very low, anything that snaps into anything else in a PC is very sensitive to dirt. When holding any type of card, including the motherboard, take care to avoid touching the card itself—always hold the edges as shown in Figure 3.

Figure 3 Handle cards gently and only on the edges

Notice that the person in the picture is holding the card by its edge as well as the metal plate, or *shim*.

Any electronic part not in a PC is exposed to ESD risk. You can reduce that risk by keeping unused pieces in anti-static bags. These bags come in an assortment of colors and sizes to store any electronic part. If an electronic device will spend any amount of time where it is at risk of ESD, drop it in an anti-static bag.

KEEPING TRACK

While ESD may be the biggest killer of PC components, another big problem is keeping track of parts. PCs come with close to 100 screws and a large number of other small parts. They also have an array of connectors that look obviously matched—until you detach them. You will save yourself time and aggravation in the long run if *before* you start undoing things, you document where the different cords are connected and where the various screws come from. That way, when you're finished and ready to go home, you can reattach everything properly the first time.

It is true that putting a screw or two in the wrong place usually will not cause any problems—but why take the chance? Following are some good strategies for working with screws.

- Reinsert screws partway back into the case holes after removing a device.
- Store the same types of screws together.
- Tape screws to the device they came from.

NEATNESS COUNTS

Keep food and beverages *away* from your PC. If you violate this rule, sooner or later you will end up with soda or donut crumbs or worse on delicate computer innards. This is not good for printed circuit boards (PCBs) and thus not good for your longevity as a tech.

TOOLS OF THE TRADE

Every tech should have basic toolkit. These toolkits are generally available at computer stores. Following are the items you should have in your toolkit and a description of what each item is used for.

Screwdrivers

- **Phillips large:** Use this screwdriver for large screws on cases and hard drives (see Figure 4).

Figure 4 Large Phillips head screwdriver

- **Phillips small:** Use this screwdriver for smaller screws on floppy drives and CD-ROMs (see Figure 5).

Figure 5 Small Phillips head screwdriver

- **Flathead large:** Use this screwdriver for the large, flathead screws on the case.
- **Flathead small:** Use this screwdriver for very few small screws (see Figure 6) and for prying things open (see Figure 7).

Figure 6 Small flathead screwdriver used on monitor connector

Figure 7 Prying loose a fan clip with a small flathead screwdriver

Hex drivers

- **Large hex:** Use this tool for case bolts.

- **Small hex:** Use this tool for card hex bolts like those on the monitor DB connector (see Figure 8).

Figure 8 Small hex driver used on monitor connector

Chip puller   Use this tool for removing ROM chips (it's mostly obsolete these days).

Grabber tool   This tool is very useful for retrieving dropped screws and holding screws for insertion, as shown in Figures 9 and 10.

FIGURE 9 The wire-grabber tool

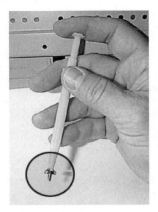

FIGURE 10 The wire-grabber tool is wonderful for picking up and positioning screws

Hemostat   This tool is also useful for holding screws, but it's especially good for gripping shunts when setting jumpers, as shown in Figure 11.

→ **Note**

This important tool is not included in most standard toolkits.

FIGURE 11 Hemostats give you a secure grip on jumper shunts

Tweezers This is another good tool for retrieving fallen screws, pulling shunts, and occasionally removing splinters.

Keeper tube Use this to hold screws, shunts, washers, standouts, and other small, easily lost bits. (The trick with this item is to actually *use* it!)

The following items are not included in standard kits but they are very useful to have on hand:

Magnifying glass This tool is for reading tiny charts on motherboards, and so on.

Magnifying reading glasses Use these glasses as an alternative to the Sherlock Holmes–style magnifying glass.

Flashlight It is often inconveniently dark even inside an open case.

Band-Aids Sooner or later you *will* cut yourself on a computer case.

Chapter 1

The Visible PC

Mastering the craft of the PC technician requires you to learn a lot of details about a zillion things. Even the most basic PC contains hundreds of discrete hardware components, each with its own set of characteristics, shapes, sizes, colors, connections, and so on. To understand the details, you often need to understand the big picture first. These labs should help you to recognize the main components of a typical PC. You will also examine all the major connectors, plugs, and sockets, and learn to recognize a particular part simply by seeing what type of connector attaches to that part.

✖ **Warning**

When you open your PC to do these exercises, you must take precautions to avoid the greatest killer of PCs: electrostatic discharge (ESD). ESD involves the passage of a static electrical charge into your PC. Have you ever rubbed a balloon against your shirt, making the balloon stick to you? That's a classic example of static electricity. If you are charged and touch your PC, you may not feel a thing, but it will! So if you skipped the Introduction, go back to it now and read up on ESD safety procedures—the life you save may be your PC's!

Lab 1.1: First Look

Objective

In this lab, you will familiarize yourself with the outside of a standard PC. At the end of this lab, you should

- Be able to identify the various buttons and drives on the front of a standard system case and the components of a standard PC keyboard

- Be able to identify the various connectors on the back of a standard system case

Setup

You need a PC for this lab, preferably a modern (less than three years old) system, although you will find some common connections on virtually any PC (even an "oldie goldie" from the early 1980s). If at all possible, try to look at a variety of computers to see what things are similar and what things are different.

Process

1. Look at the front of your system unit. You will probably have an On/Off button or switch and a Reset button. (Don't panic if there's no Reset button—not all systems have them. Also, on some older PCs the On/Off switch is on the back.)

2. Your system should also have an opening for floppy disks and, unless it's an older PC, a tray that slides out to receive your CD-ROMs (see Figure 1-1). There should also be several LEDs that light up when the hard drive or other device is accessed.

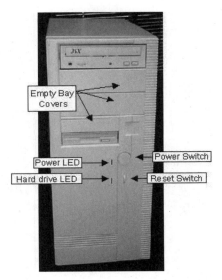

FIGURE 1-1 Can you locate the floppy drive and CD-ROM drive on this unit?

3. Now look at the back of the system unit. You probably see lots of cables and wires, each one leading to a special connector on the back of the unit. Some will be "male" (connectors with pins), and some will be "female" (connectors with holes). Each connector has a specific number of pins or holes that matches a specific device connected to the system unit.

✖ Warning

Shut off the power to your system and *unplug* your PC from the wall socket before doing the following exercise.

4. Take a look at the connections one at a time, and try plugging and unplugging the cable that is attached to each. Make sure you look at the connections to the system unit *and* to the device at the other end of the cable.

5.   Make note of which connectors and cables go with which devices. If possible, do this for more than one system unit.

_____

_____

_____

_____

6.   Now let's look at one of the two most important human interfaces on a PC: the keyboard. (You'll study monitors in more detail when you do the video labs.)

Look at the way your keyboard is laid out. For the most part it looks like a typewriter keyboard (for those of you old enough to remember typewriters!), but with some extra keys.

At the top left-hand corner is the ESC key.

Moving to the right are the function keys (F1 through F12). Each of these keys has special uses that I'll discuss as I get to that function.

To the right of the F12 key are the PRINT SCREEN, SCROLL LOCK, and PAUSE/BREAK keys.

At the top of the next row of keys are the numeric keys and special characters. Starting at the left, you'll find the tilde (~), number/symbol keys, and finally the BACKSPACE key.

The subsequent rows follow the classic QWERTY keyboard layout familiar to touch typists everywhere, with the addition of keys labeled CTRL (control), ALT, and on some Microsoft keyboards, a Windows symbol and a Menu symbol.

The navigation area of the keyboard is to the right of the main typing area. To the right of the BACKSPACE key is a group of six special function keys: INSERT, DELETE, HOME, END, PAGE UP, and PAGE DOWN. Right below those six keys you normally find the arrow keys, which you can use instead of a mouse to move around.

Finally, on the right side of the keyboard is the numeric keypad.

7. The two system units in Figure 1-2 look different, but they have many connectors in common. Try to find the following connectors on each system unit:

    ● Power

    ● Monitor

    ● Mouse

    ● Keyboard

    ● Printer

    ● Network

FIGURE 1-2 Can you match the connectors on these two system units?

Lab 1.2: Exterior Connections

Objective

In this lab, you will identify the external connections on a standard PC. At the end of this lab, you should

    ● Be able to identify the external connectors on a PC

    ● Know the function of each external connection

    ● Understand how to handle external connections

Setup

You need a PC for this lab, preferably a modern (less than three years old) system. If at all possible, try to look at a variety of computers to compare similarities and differences.

> ✖ **Warning**
>
> *Shut off* the power to your system and *unplug* your PC from the wall socket before doing this exercise.

Process

> ➜ **Note**
>
> Before you disconnect a cable, *look* at it carefully and make a note of where it plugs in so you can reattach it in the correct place.

1. After shutting off the power, unplug your PC's cables and plug them back in until you get a feel for how snugly they fit and how almost every cable has its own distinct socket to plug into.

2. Remove or disconnect any of the following cables from your system:

    - AC power cord from the back of the PC power supply and power strip

    - AC power cord from the back of the monitor (if detachable) and power strip

    - Data cable from the monitor to the PC

    - Data cable from the printer to the PC (both ends)

    - Data cable from the speakers to the PC

    - Data cable from the keyboard to the PC

    - Data cable from the mouse to the PC

    - Data network cable from the PC

    - Data cable (telephone wire) from the modem to the telephone jack

3. If you are working with someone else, play "Flash Cords." Have your partner hold up various cables. Try to guess what they connect to by the connectors on the ends. Then switch roles with your partner.

4. Examine other computers to see if they have different connectors than the one you have been working with. See if you can identify the peripherals that connect to those sockets.

5. Fill in the connector type(s) that matches each cable type.

Cable Type	Connector Type(s)
Keyboard cable	_____
Mouse cable	_____
Speaker cable	_____
Monitor data cable	_____
Printer data cable (printer end)	_____
Printer data cable (case end)	_____
Network data cable	_____
Modem/telephone wire	_____

6. Identify the connectors pictured below. What is the name of each connector and what does it connect to?

_____
_____

_____
_____

_____
_____

_____
_____

_____
_____

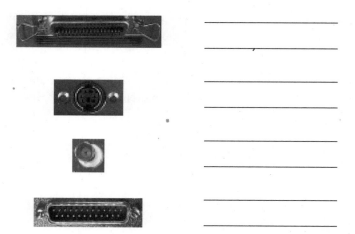

Lab 1.3: Internal Components

Objective

In this lab, you will identify the internal components of a standard PC. At the end of this lab, you should

- Recognize all of the major components inside a PC

- Be able to name the function of each component

- Understand what components relate to what external connections

Setup

Place the computer you are going to use on a flat, stable surface (preferably on a static pad) where you can sit or stand comfortably to inspect the insides. Using proper ESD procedures, open the case and lay the computer down so the open side faces the ceiling.

✖ **Warning**

Shut off the power on your system and *unplug* your PC from the wall socket before doing this exercise.

Process

1. Take the cover off your system, using either a large Phillips screwdriver or a large hex driver to remove the retaining screws. Then take a look at the inside of your PC. What do you see? Lots of cables and wires, for starters (see Figure 1-3). Most of them originate at the power supply and terminate at various devices. You may have to move some of them in order to see the motherboard, but remember your ESD procedures and be *gentle*. Sometimes the slightest bump is enough to unseat a connection.

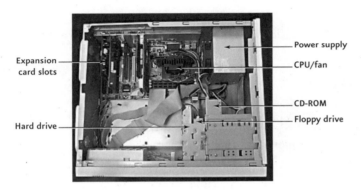

FIGURE 1-3 Inside a PC

2. Look in your PC and see if you can locate the CPU chip.

    Is it under a fan? If so, is the fan permanently attached? If the fan isn't permanently attached, *carefully* remove it after you review the ESD procedures in the Introduction. Make a note of the type of chip you have.

    If you are in a computer lab, examine a number of different CPU chips. Notice where on the motherboard you find them.

3. Look in your PC and find the RAM modules.

    Make a note of the type you have.

    Again, if possible, look at several different PCs, preferably both older and newer models.

4.   Now look in your PC and find the expansion slots.

Note the number and type(s) of slots you have in your machine.

_____

_____

Some of the expansion slots should have cards in them—probably modem cards, sound cards, and video cards.

Note which expansion cards are installed in your PC, and look at the external connectors on each.

_____

5.   Locate the large silver box that is the power supply.

Trace the wires leading out of it. Remember to be *gentle*.

Find the power plug for the motherboard. Does it look like the one in Figure 1-4? If you have a newer PC, it probably will; if you have an older PC, it might not.

FIGURE 1-4 Power plug for the motherboard

Find the power connections for the floppy, CD-ROM (if there is one), and hard drives. Do they look like one of the connectors in Figure 1-5? They should!

6.   Now look at the floppy drive. It should have a flat ribbon cable attached to it.

Trace the cable to the motherboard. If you can, do this on several computers. Do the same for the hard drive and for the CD-ROM drive, if present.

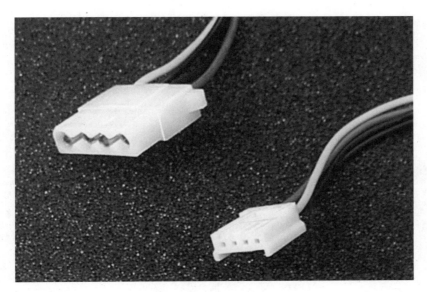

FIGURE 1-5 Power connectors

These cables are about 1.5 inches in width, and they are usually gray with a colored stripe on one side. The stripe—usually red—orients the cable properly to the connections on the motherboard and the drive.

The cable to the floppy drive has 34 wires, and it also has a unique feature: A portion of the cable has a twist in the center. This twist is seven wires wide and enables you to determine by its position relative to the twist whether a floppy drive will be designated drive A: or (normally not relevant on modern systems) drive B:.

The cable that connects the hard drive(s) and the CD-ROM drive to the motherboard has 40 wires and no twist. It does have a different color edge on one side for orientation, however.

7. After noting their current state, disconnect and reconnect each device's cable in turn. Practice this a few times with each device. Try to put the cable back on the device backward. Make sure that the cables are properly connected when you've finished.

8. Take a look at where the cables are connected to the motherboard. Make note of the proper cable orientation. Practice disconnecting and reconnecting the cables to the motherboard. Do you have any problems if you try to connect these backward?

9. See if you can locate any jumpers or DIP switches on your motherboard. Resist the temptation to play with them at this point—just make a note of what you find. In particular, look for the identifying labels on the motherboard.

_____

10. Identify the components in Figure 1-6.

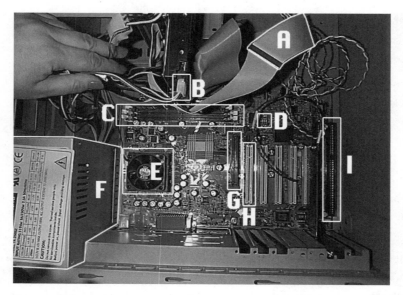

FIGURE 1-6 Do you recognize these components inside your PC?

A _____

B _____

C _____

D _____

E _____

F _____

G _____

H _____

I _____

Chapter 2
Microprocessors

For all practical purposes, the terms *microprocessor* and *central processing unit* (CPU) mean the same thing: They describe that big chip inside your computer that many people say is the brain of the system. However, comparing a CPU to a human brain greatly overstates its capabilities. A CPU functions more like a very powerful calculator than a brain—but, oh, what a calculator! Today's CPUs add, subtract, multiply, and divide millions of numbers per second. It's simply the speed of the CPU, rather than actual intelligence, that enables computers to perform feats such as accessing the Internet, playing visually stunning games, or creating graphics.

CPU makers name their microprocessors in a fashion similar to the way automobile manufacturers name cars: CPU names include a make and a model, such as Intel Pentium or AMD Duron. You probably already know what a CPU looks like—invariably covered by some huge fan or heat sink, a CPU stands out inside the case. A good PC technician needs to be familiar with types of CPUs and sockets in order to support PCs well.

Lab 2.1: Microprocessors

Objective

In this lab, you will practice identifying CPUs and CPU fan components. At the end of this lab, you should

- Recognize the different kinds of CPUs

- Know the basic features of different classes of CPUs

- Recognize different CPU fan attachments

Setup

This lab works best if you have access to a variety of CPUs, but you should at least have access to some kind of Pentium chip.

> ✖ **Warning**
>
> When you are holding a CPU chip, take extra care not to touch any of the chip's connectors, including the pins on a socket chip and the plates on a slot chip. Remember to follow proper ESD procedures.

Process

1. Look at the chips pictured in Figure 2-1, making note of the differences you see, especially with regard to the bottom views. Compare the chips in the image to yours. If possible, compare the chips in the image to chips in a variety of computers.

_____

_____

FIGURE 2-1 Different CPU chips

2. There are many different types of fans, each of which is attached to a CPU in a different way. Just to make things more complicated, manufacturers frequently produce new kinds of fans. There are a couple of very common fan types that are worth reviewing here.

    Screw-down This type of fan has two separate parts: the base and the fan itself. The base normally attaches to the CPU, using grooves or latches on the bottom to hold it in place. The base has a large circular opening at the top with screw grooves on the inside. The fan is designed to screw into this opening, eventually pressing against the chip underneath to hold the fan securely in place.

Clip   This type of fan comes in one piece, with the heat sink and fan combined. The clip is actually a piece of metal running through the center of the heat sink with metal loops on either end that fit over small protrusions on the socket to hold the fan assembly in place. There are two clip-fan types.

> **With hinge**   This type of clip has a small hinge on one side that makes attaching and removing the fan easier. To remove the fan, simply push down on the hinged clip and it magically pops off the protrusion, allowing you to raise the fan assembly up and work it off the other protrusion.

> **Without hinge**   This type of clip has—you guessed it—no hinge. This isn't a problem when you attach the fan, although you often have to exert more pressure than seems desirable to get the little hooks over the little bumps. However, removing the fan can be problematic. To do so, you must push down on one of the connectors while you pry it off the protrusion with a small screwdriver (see Figure 2-2).

FIGURE 2-2 Prying off a clip fan with a small flathead screwdriver

3.   Look at the fans in Figure 2-3. Can you identify the different attachment types? Which type(s) do you have?

4.   CPU fans have an additional feature: an electrical connection to provide power, either directly from the power supply (a Molex connector) or through a small shunt-like connector that attaches to the motherboard (see Figure 2-4). (The latter connection is more common than the former.) Find the fan power connection and practice disconnecting and reconnecting it.

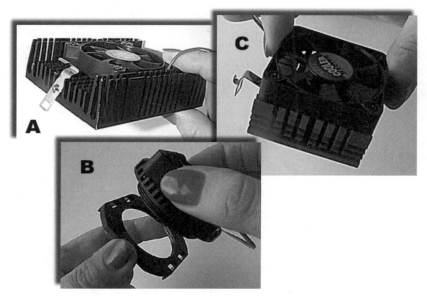

Figure 2-3 Different CPU fans

Figure 2-4 Fan power connection on a motherboard

5. Fill in the number of data and address bus bits (wires) for each CPU in the following chart.

CPU	External Data Bus Bits	Address Bus Bits
Intel 8086		
Intel 8088		
Intel 80286		
Intel 80386DX		
Intel 80386SX		
AMD AM386DX		
AMD AM386SX		
Intel 80486DX		
AMD AM486DX		
Intel Pentium		
AMD Athlon		
AMD Duron		
Intel Pentium Pro		
Intel Pentium II		
Intel Pentium III		

6. See how many of the chip features you can fill in knowing the maker and CPU type.

	Maker	CPU Type	Package	Bus Speed (MHz)	Cache L1 (KB)	L2 (KB)	Clock Speed Multiplier
A	Intel	Pentium III 750					
B	AMD	Athlon 600					
C	AMD	Duron 800					

	Maker	CPU Type	Package	Bus Speed (MHz)	Cache L1 (KB)	L2 (KB)	Clock Speed Multiplier
D	Intel	Celeron 566	_____	_____	_____	_____	_____
E	AMD	K6-2 475	_____	_____	_____	_____	_____
F	Intel	Pentium II 450	_____	_____	_____	_____	_____

7. Identify the fan types shown in Figure 2-3 (screw-down, hinged clip, or plain clip).

Fan	Type
1	_____
2	_____
3	_____

Lab 2.2: Socket City

Objective

In this lab, you will identify and use various CPU sockets. At the end of this lab, you should

- Recognize different kinds of CPU sockets
- Know which CPUs need which sockets

Setup

This lab works best if you have multiple PCs or at least multiple motherboards with different sockets.

Process

1. Examine the CPU socket on your motherboard. If you have access to multiple examples, look at each in turn and note the differences. If there is no chip in the motherboard (you'll learn about chip removal in Lab 2.3), examine the mechanisms that hold the chip in place.

2. Identify the different socket types in Figure 2-5.

    A _____

    B _____

    C _____

    D _____

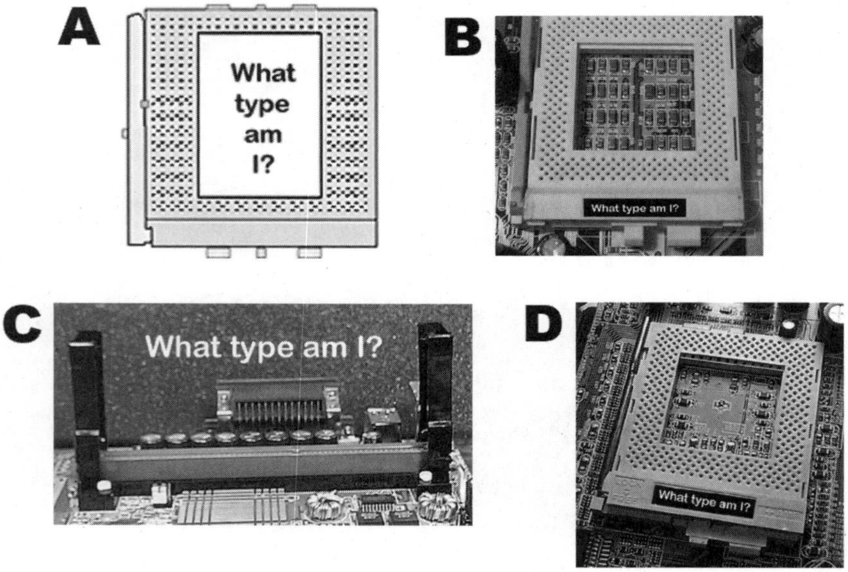

FIGURE 2-5 Identify these sockets

3. Test your knowledge of chip/socket pairs. Draw a line connecting each CPU with its corresponding socket type.

CPU	Socket Type
Pentium P54C	Socket 370
Pentium Pro	Slot 1
Celeron (II) 600	Socket A
Athlon 1200	Socket 8
Pentium II	Socket 7

Lab 2.3: CPU Installation

Objective

In this lab, you will practice removing and installing a CPU and CPU fan components. At the end of this lab, you should

- Be able to remove and install a CPU safely and correctly

- Be able to remove and install a CPU fan safely and correctly

Setup

This lab requires a motherboard with an appropriate (matching) CPU chip and fan. Remember to follow proper ESD procedures. You should, if possible, practice on different types of computers.

✖ **Warning**

> Remember not to mess with anyone else's computer unless you can afford to replace it. Opening the case is fine, but removing and installing CPUs requires practice before risking damage to expensive machines.

Process

1. Start with the computer case open and the power off, using proper ESD procedures. Examine the CPU in your system.

    First, notice how the CPU is placed and what sort of fan/fan attachments it uses. Make a note of this information.

    _____

    Determine the chip type and the interface type.

    _____

    Does your CPU use a socket or a slot? _____

    What type of socket or slot does it use? _____

✔ **Tech Note**

Socket interfaces usually tell you their type if you look. Remember that interfaces for Pentium CPUs come in a variety of flavors: Socket 7, Socket 8, Socket 370, Slot 1, Slot A, and Socket A.

2. If possible, find a system with a socket for a PGA-type chip and remove the fan. (You have to remove the fan before you can remove the chip.)

Once you have removed the fan, look at the underside. It should be coated with a white paste known as *heat dope*. Whether your fan is of the screw-down or clip variety, you should apply some heat dope to the surface that contacts the CPU. Heat dope comes in a tube, and when applied it makes an unbroken seal between the CPU chip and the fan's heat sink, facilitating better heat extraction.

3. Now try removing the CPU chip.

✖ **Warning**

Be careful to remove the CPU straight up, not at an angle. If you remove a CPU at an angle, you will bend the tiny pins. Notice the orientation of the CPU's notched edge. Almost all CPUs have them.

Socket-type CPUs   To remove a socket-type CPU, move the zero insertion force (ZIF) lever a little outward to clear the safety notch, and then raise it to a perpendicular position. Next, grasp the chip carefully by its edges and lift it straight up out of the socket. Be very careful not to move the chip sideways at all, or you will bend the pins. Also make sure that the lever stays in an upright position.

SEC-type CPUs   Removing single-edged cartridge (SEC) CPU chips that use a slot interface normally does not require removing the fan, which is usually attached to the chip cartridge itself. To remove a slot CPU, first check for and release any retaining clips that may be securing it to the slot, and then grasp the cartridge firmly on both ends and pull straight up from the motherboard.

4. Now that you have the CPU chip out, examine it closely. The manufacturer usually prints the chip's brand and type directly on the chip, providing you with some important facts about the chip's design and performance capabilities. If your chip is an Intel Celeron II 600, for example, you know that its PGA packaging fits in a Socket 370, its bus speed is 66 MHz, and it runs at 600 MHz. Make a note of the relevant specs for your chip.

_____

_____

5. Reinsert the CPU and reattach the fan.

6. Turn your system back on to make sure you got the CPU seated properly.

   Don't forget to plug the fan back in.

Chapter 3
RAM

Random-access memory (RAM) is the working memory of your PC. Any device that can hold data is memory. Random access means that any part of the memory can be accessed with equal ease. Due to its low cost, high speed, and capability to contain a lot of data in a relatively small package, dynamic random-access memory (DRAM) is the standard RAM used in all computers today. Even Macintoshes and mainframes use DRAM. In fact, you can find DRAM in just about everything today, from automobiles to automatic bread makers.

DRAM usually manifests itself as a number of chips soldered onto a card of some type. When you load a program, the program copies it from the mass storage device (usually a hard drive, but it could be a floppy disk, a CD-ROM disk, or some other device that can hold values when the computer is turned off) to RAM and then runs. If the RAM isn't right, nothing is. The following labs are designed to give you practice working with RAM, both physically (installing RAM) and mentally (calculating volumes and banking).

Lab 3.1: RAM Identification and Installation

Objective

In this lab, you will practice removing and installing RAM. At the end of this lab, you should

- Recognize the different kinds of RAM sticks
- Be able to remove and install RAM safely and correctly

Setup

This lab requires a working computer with RAM installed. If you are in a computer lab or you have access to multiple PCs, you should practice on as many different PCs as possible.

Process

1. Examine the RAM on your motherboard. Your motherboard most likely has one of the following three types of RAM.

    30-pin SIMMs   These are about three inches long and have 30 physical pins (connector plates).

    72-pin SIMMs   These are about four inches long and have 72 physical pins (connector plates); these SIMMs have one notch on bottom that is offset slightly.

    168-pin DIMMs   DIMMs are about five inches long and have 84 physical pins (connector plates). These DIMMs have two notches on the bottom: one centered and the other offset a quarter of the length from one end.

    Note the type of RAM your motherboard requires. _____

    How many banks of RAM are there on your system? _____

2. Review the ESD and component-handling instructions. Practice removing and installing the RAM sticks as follows.

Installation

a.   30-pin SIMMs

    1)   Slide it into its slots at a 45-degree angle.

        One side is notched for orientation.

        If it doesn't fit correctly, do not force it—turn it around.

    2)   Once the stick is correctly inserted into the slot, pop it up so it's perpendicular to the board.

        You should hear a click as the holders on either side pop into place.

    3)   When setting several RAM sticks in a bank, work in stages to insert and then snap in the sticks (that is, sock-sock-shoe-shoe, not sock-shoe-sock-shoe), starting at one side and working across to the other.

        (a)   Put every stick you plan to insert in its slot at an angle.

        (b)   When all the sticks are in, pop them up in order starting with the one on top so that you don't crowd the ones behind it that are still at an angle.

b.   72-pin SIMMs

    1)   The notch in the bottom of 72-pin SIMMs is the orientation key, as it is offset slightly from the center.

    2)   Place the 72-pin SIMM into the slot so it leans sideways at a 45-degree angle.

        Make sure the notch is correctly positioned.

        (a)   The ends of the SIMM will rock back and forth if you have it in backward.

        (b)   Do not use a Dremel tool to adjust the notch—turn the stick around if it doesn't fit.

    3)   Once the stick is correctly inserted into the slot, pop it up so it's perpendicular to the board.

        You should hear a click as the holders on either side pop into place.

    4)   When setting several RAM sticks in a bank, work in stages to insert and then snap in the sticks (that is, sock-sock-shoe-shoe, not sock-shoe-sock-shoe), starting at one side of the bank and working across to the other.

        (a)   Put every stick you plan to insert into its slot at a 45-degree angle.

(b) When all the sticks are in, pop them up in order starting with the one on top so that you don't crowd the ones behind it that are still at an angle.

c.   168-pin DIMMs

   1)   There are two orientation notches in the DIMM: one is centered and the other is offset a quarter of the length from one end.

   2)   Check the side latches on the slot where you are about to place the DIMM.

         The latches should be in the down position (closest to the board).

   3)   Place the DIMM in the slot perpendicular to the board, keeping in mind the orientation notches.

   4)   When you know the DIMM is properly placed, push straight down on the DIMM using the heel of your hand until your hear the side latches click into place.

         The latches should now be in the up position, indicating the DIMM is properly seated in the slot.

Removal

a.   30-pin and 72-pin SIMMs

   1)   Find the holders on both sides of the individual SIMM.

   2)   With your fingers, push the holders away from the ends of the SIMM, staying on the same vertical plane as the SIMM (in other words, the holders drop down and away like the door of a mailbox).

         When the holders are released far enough, the SIMM will pop down sideways to a 45-degree angle.

   3)   You can now lift the SIMM easily from its slot.

b.   168-pin DIMM

   1)   Find the latches at either side of the DIMM slot.

   2)   With your fingers, press straight down on the latches.

         The latches should move with a minimum of resistance to the down position.

   3)   When the latches reach the down position, the DIMM should pop out of the slot like toast from a toaster.

3. After reinstalling the RAM, boot up the system. Watch the RAM count. Does the PC still see all of the RAM?

✔ **Tech Note**

If your system has any problems when you reboot, remember that you must turn off the power and unplug the computer before reseating the RAM.

---

4. Identify the RAM sticks in Figure 3-1 and match them with the appropriate slots in the image. Record the type and description of each and enter the matching slot number.

	Type/Description	Matching Slot #
A	_____	_____
B	_____	_____
C	_____	_____

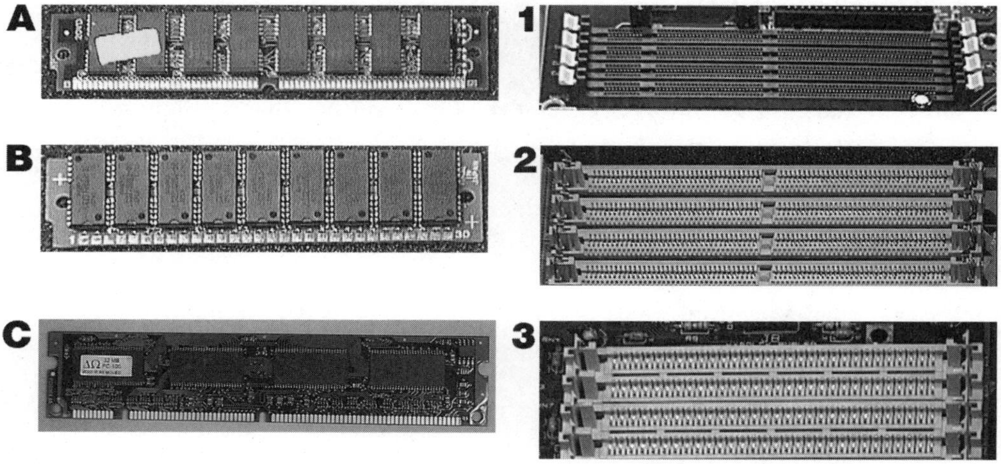

FIGURE 3-1 RAM sticks and slots

Lab 3.2: RAM Banking and Volume

Objective

In this lab, you will calculate RAM. At the end of this lab, you should

- Be able to calculate the number of SIMMs/DIMMs needed to make a bank in a particular CPU
- Be able to calculate the volume of a stick of RAM

Setup

This lab requires only a working brain.

Process

1. When it comes to banking RAM, keep the following things in mind.

   SIMMs and DIMMs come in unique widths.

   - 30-pin SIMM = 8 bits
   - 72-pin SIMM = 32 bits
   - 168-pin DIMM = 64 bits

   The external data bus (EDB) of each of the CPU "families" has a unique width.

   - 8088 = 8 bits
   - 8086 = 16 bits
   - 286 = 16 bits
   - 386DX = 32 bits
   - 386SX = 16 bits
   - 486 = 32 bits
   - Pentium = 64 bits

   The RAM must occupy the *entire* width of the EDB.

   As a result, the formula to determine banking is

   1 bank = width of the EDB / width of the SIMM or DIMM

2.   Using the preceding formula, fill in the blanks to complete the following examples.

   a.   How many 30-pin SIMMs does it take to make a bank on a 386DX?

        Take the width of a 30-pin SIMM (____bits) and divide it into the width of the EDB of a 386DX (____ bits).

        ____ ÷ ____ = ____

        It takes _____ 30-pin SIMMs to make a bank on a 386DX.

   b.   How many 72-pin SIMMs does it take to make a bank on a Pentium?

        Take the width of a 72-pin SIMM (____bits) and divide it into the width of the EDB of a Pentium (____bits).

        ____ ÷ ____ = ____

        It takes _____ 72-pin SIMMs to make a bank on a Pentium.

   c.   How many 168-pin DIMMs does it take to make a bank on a Pentium?

        Take the width of a DIMM (____bits) and divide it into the width of the EDB of a Pentium (____bits).

        ____ ÷ ____ = ____

        It takes _____ DIMMs to make a bank on a Pentium.

   d.   How many 72-pin SIMMs does it take to make a bank on a 386SX?

        Take the width of the SIMM (____bits) and divide it into the width of the EDB of a 386SX (____bits).

        ____ ÷ ____ = ____

        It takes _____ SIMMs to make a bank on a 386SX.

➜ **Note**

Think very carefully about this one!

3. To determine the volume of RAM, think of RAM as being a giant spreadsheet with columns and rows.

The spreadsheet's columns represent the "width" of the RAM. Remember that SIMMs and DIMMs come in unique widths. These widths are the amount of information that the RAM can send down the EDB at one time.

30-pin SIMM = 8 bits

72-pin SIMM = 32 bits

168-pin DIMM = 64 bits

The spreadsheet's rows represent the "depth" of the RAM. These rows are represented in multiples of megabits (Mb). One megabit = 1,048,576 bits.

A stick of RAM is referenced using the form "depth times width."

1 × 8

1Mb depth (or 1,048,576 rows) times 8 bits (8 bits = 1 byte) across

This tells us it is a 30-pin SIMM (8 bits wide), and the total volume is 1MB.

1 × 32

1Mb depth times 32 bits across

This tells us it is a 72-pin SIMM (32 bits wide) and that the total volume is 4MB.

You can find out how many bytes are present by dividing 8 bits into 32 bits. The answer is 4 bytes. Then multiply that answer (4 bytes) by the depth (1Mb) to get a total volume of 4MB for a 1 × 32 SIMM.

4. Fill in the blanks to complete the following exercises.

a. 4 × 32

____ Mb depth times ____ bits across

This tells us it is a _____ and that the total volume is ____ MB.

Find out how many bytes are present by dividing ____ bits into ____ bits. The answer is ____ bytes. Then multiply that answer (____ bytes) by the depth (____ Mb) to get a total volume of ____ MB for a 4 × 32 SIMM.

b. 4×64

____ Mb depth times ____ bits across

This tells us it is a _____ and that the total volume is ____ MB.

Find out how many bytes are present by dividing ____ bits into ____ bits. The answer is ____ bytes. Then multiply that answer (____ bytes) by the depth (____ Mb) to get a total volume of ____ MB for a 4×64 DIMM.

5.   Review the following sample problems until you are sure you understand how to calculate banking and volumes.

a.   You have a Pentium system with open 72-pin RAM slots. The system has 64MB on it at this point, and you want to add another 32MB using 72-pin SIMMs. What do you need to add?

1)   First, figure out how many SIMMs it takes to make a bank on a Pentium system.

72-pin SIMMs are 32 bits wide, and a Pentium EDB is 64 bits wide.

32 goes into 64 twice, so you need 2 SIMMs to make a bank.

2)   Next, calculate the volume of each stick (remember that all the sticks in a bank must be identical). You want to add a total of 32MB of RAM using two sticks, so each stick should have a volume of 16MB.

$32 \div 2 = 16$

3)   However, you can't go into the store and ask for two 16MB 72-pin SIMMs. If you want to be understood, you have to use RAM talk: "I want one 4×8 SIMM, please." You know the second number (32), but you must calculate the depth (the X in $X \times 32$). What multiplied by 32 equals the 16MB volume you've calculated for each stick?

Divide 8 bits (1 byte) into the 32-bit width of the 72-pin SIMM to get the number of bytes.

$32 \div 8 = 4$

The SIMM is 4 bytes wide.

What times 4 equals 16? Answer: 4.

You need two 4×32 sticks to get an additional 32MB of RAM using 72-pin SIMMs.

    b.   You have an older 486 motherboard that has an open bank of 30-pin slots. You have a handful of 2 × 8 SIMMs. How much RAM will you add to the system if you fill the bank with these 2 × 8s?

       1)   First figure out how many SIMMs you need to fill the bank.

          30-pin SIMMs are 8 bits wide, and the EDB of a 486 is 32 bits wide:

$$32 \div 8 = 4$$

          You will need four 2 × 8 sticks to fill the bank.

       2)   Figure out how much volume each of the sticks has.

          Divide 8 bits into the width of the SIMM to get the number of bytes:

$$8 \div 8 = 1$$

          So each stick is 1 byte wide.

          Multiply 1 byte by the depth (2MB) to get the volume of the stick:

$$1 \times 2 = 2$$

          Each stick has a volume of 2MB.

          Multiply the number of sticks by their volume:

$$4 \times 2 = 8$$

    You've added 8MB of RAM to this system.

6.   Fill in the chart below. See how much you can do from memory.

Banking Formula	One Bank in a 386	One Bank in a 486	One Bank in a Pentium	One Bank in a Pentium II	One Bank in a Pentium III
30-pin SIMM	_____	_____	_____	_____	_____
72-pin SIMM	_____	_____	_____	_____	_____
168-pin DIMM	_____	_____	_____	_____	_____

7. Using what you learned in the preceding volume and banking exercises, try to complete the following problems.

    a.   You have a Pentium system that has 128MB of RAM and two open DIMM slots. You want to add another 128MB of RAM and leave a slot available for expansion in the future. What do you need to add to your system?

        1)   Knowing that it only takes one DIMM for a bank on a Pentium, you know you will need a **X** $\times$ 64 for the system.

                Divide ____ bits into the ____ bits to get bytes for the stick. You get ____.

                What times ____ equals 128? ____ $\times$ ____ = 128.

        2)   You will need ____ ____ $\times$ ____ stick(s) to add 128MB of RAM to this system.

        3)   Do you still have an available slot? Yes/No

    b.   You have a Pentium system with DIMMs in it equaling 160MB of RAM. You pull one stick and sell it to a friend. Your system now tallies 128MB of RAM. What did you sell your friend?

        1)   Figure out the size of the stick.

                ____ – ____ = ____ MB

        2)   ____ $\times$ ____ will equal ____ MB.

                Divide ____ bits into ____ bits to get bytes and you get ____.

                Divide ____ bytes into the ____ bytes to get ____.

        3)   You sold your friend a ____ $\times$ ____.

        Hope you got a decent price!

Chapter 4

Motherboards and BIOS

Everybody who has used a computer for any amount of time has had to boot it, but a PC tech needs to know this process in detail and be able to troubleshoot it when something goes wrong. In this chapter, you will learn about the boot process and create some POST errors.

Lab 4.1 focuses on the software/firmware that handles critical functions for the devices you attach to your motherboard: the system ROM, BIOS, and CMOS. In particular, you will work with the CMOS setup utility that is used to configure certain types of hardware, such as RAM, hard drives, and floppy drives. Critical information that describes these devices is stored on a separate, special RAM chip called a CMOS (complementary metal-oxide semiconductor) chip.

To most techs, the concept of adding or replacing a motherboard can be extremely intimidating. It really shouldn't be. Motherboard installation is a common and necessary part of PC repair, although it can sometimes be a little tedious and messy due to the large number of parts involved. You will step through the process of motherboard removal and installation and learn about motherboard layouts and manuals.

Lab 4.1: System ROM, BIOS, CMOS, and Other Tools

Objective

In this lab, you will identify the system ROM, clock, and CMOS chip; practice using Device Manager, SYSEDIT, and REGEDIT; and work with the CMOS setup utility to configure the changeable BIOS. At the end of this lab, you should

- Be able to find the system ROM, CMOS chip, and clock on any motherboard

- Know how to use Device Manager, SYSEDIT, and REGEDIT

- Be able to configure the changeable BIOS using the CMOS setup utility

Setup

This lab requires at least one working computer running Windows 9x that you can open to look at the motherboard. As usual, if you have access to more than one system, take advantage of it.

Process

1. First locate your system ROM.

   Following proper ESD procedures, open your case and look at your motherboard.

   There should be a chip on the motherboard about 1½-inches long and about ½-inch wide. There should be a holographic tag on the top of it as well, which may have one of the following labels:

   - AMIBIOS

   - AWARD

   - Phoenix

The chip could even be proprietary to the maker of your computer and have a completely different tag. The three tags listed previously are the most common.

This chip is your system ROM (see Figure 4-1). It stores programs known as *firmware*.

FIGURE 4-1 System ROM

2. Find the battery on your motherboard. Batteries come in many flavors, as shown in Figure 4-2.

FIGURE 4-2 Three types of batteries

On older motherboards, the battery may be barrel-shaped and soldered directly onto the motherboard.

The battery might be a silver, circular disk held in place with a clip.

The battery might be in a black rectangular box with a picture of a clock and the word "DALLAS" or "ODIN" printed on it.

These batteries keep volatile BIOS valid.

3.   Using proper ESD procedures, close up your case and reboot your system.

✖ Warning

The tools you will be working with in this lab can seriously screw up your system, so before you start, *make sure* you have reviewed some good explanatory material on device drivers and on the use of Device Manager, SYSEDIT, and REGEDIT (32), and you feel comfortable using them.

---

4.   Open Device Manager on your system.

     Examine the devices on your system, and make a note of the devices present.

     _____

     _____

     _____

     _____

5.   Close Device Manager.

6.   Run SYSEDIT.

     Check the contents of your SYSTEM.INI, WIN.INI, CONFIG.SYS, and (if you have one) AUTOEXEC.BAT files.

     Try editing your CONFIG.SYS file—just be sure not to save your changes!

7.   Close SYSEDIT without saving any changes you made.

8.   Run REGEDIT.

     Look at the contents of the different HKEY folders. Try to see what sort of information each is used for.

     Think of working with the Registry as sort of like handling a chainsaw. It's very powerful in experienced hands, but it's potentially devastating in the inexperienced ones. You will learn more about the Registry in later chapters, but for now just look.

9. Now you are going to work with the "changeable" BIOS stored on the CMOS chip, using the CMOS setup utility. Look again at Figure 4-2. The battery with "DALLAS" and the picture of a clock on it is actually also the CMOS chip—it performs both functions.

   a. To begin this exercise, enter the CMOS setup program by pressing the appropriate key while (re)booting your system.

      On some systems it is very easy to enter CMOS setup. Watch the screen during the boot process—your system may prompt you to press a specific key. Didn't catch it? You can try guessing. Unfortunately, there are quite a few possibilities.

      - Press DELETE during the boot process.

      - Press F2 during the boot process.

      - Press F10 during the boot process.

      - Press CTRL-ALT-INSERT during the boot process.

      - Press CTRL-A during the boot process.

      - Press CTRL-F1 during the boot process.

      Only one of these options will be right for your system. If you're not sure and you can't spot the instructions as they scroll by, at least try pressing DELETE and the different Function keys. You can try to press more than one key during a single boot as long as you press them during the part of the boot process when your system is expecting this input.

      If none of these options works on your system, you can cheat and look it up in your handy-dandy motherboard manual, if you have one.

      By the way, you should *always* keep your motherboard manual, as it comes in handy very often.

      You could also go to the PC manufacturer's Web site and poke around until you find the right keystrokes to get into your system's CMOS setup program.

      While you are there, download the motherboard manual, because if you got to this step, you didn't have it for the previous instructions.

   b. Once you have entered the CMOS setup program, look at the screen and compare it to Figures 4-3 and 4-4. The important point here is that while the screens for different CMOS setup programs may look different, they all have the same functions.

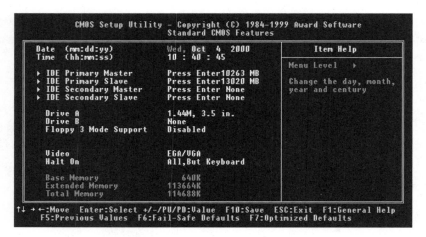

FIGURE 4-3 Award BIOS Standard CMOS Features screen

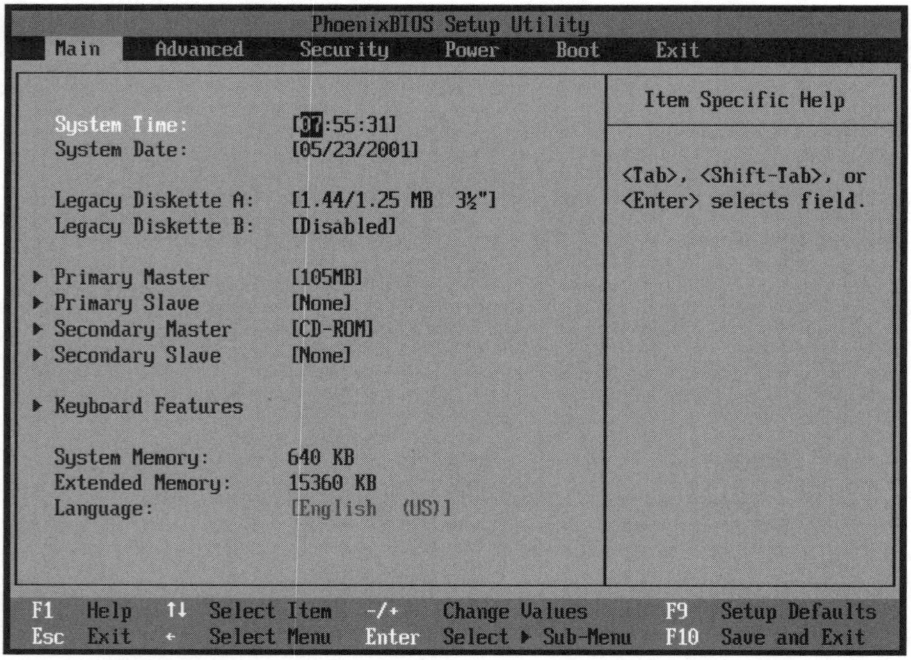

FIGURE 4-4 Phoenix BIOS Main screen

The CMOS setup program controls the "changeable" BIOS—that is, things on your system you can change, such as

- Date

- Time

- Hard drives

- Floppy drives

- Boot sequence

- RAM

- Serial and parallel port assignments

c. Look at the settings and the different screens in your CMOS program and make a note of them.

1) Date_____

Is the date correct?_____

Change the date to a week in the future and then change it back.

2) Time _____

Is the time accurate?_____

How would you change it?_____

3) Hard drives _____

Can you find the number of cylinders?_____

Heads?_____

Sectors?_____

4) Floppy drives _____

What type of floppy drive do you have set up?_____

Is it set to the A: drive or the B: drive?_____

Do you have both? _____

5) Boot sequence _____

How is your boot sequence set?_____

6) RAM _____

   How much RAM does your system have? _____

   How much is base memory? _____

   How much is extended memory? _____

7) Serial and parallel port assignments _____

   How many serial ports do you have? _____

   What are their assignments? _____

   How many parallel ports do you have? _____

   What are their assignments? _____

8) Do you have a virus warning? _____

   Is it enabled or disabled? _____

→ **Note**

The virus warning in CMOS alerts the user if changes are to be made in the boot sector of the hard drive.

---

9) Find the Swap Floppy Device option.

   Is it enabled or disabled? _____

10) Do you have a CPU Soft Menu option? _____

    What is the motherboard speed? _____

    What is the multiplier factor? _____

11) Look around at some of the other options, but be careful not to change any.

12) Read the screens to find out how you exit your CMOS program, and then do it.

→ **Note**

Commands are often listed at the bottom of the screen.

Lab 4.2: POST and the Boot Process

Objective

In this lab, you will generate POST errors and step through the boot process. At the end of this lab, you should

- Be able to recognize POST errors when they occur

- Be familiar with the steps in the DOS/Windows 9x boot process and the method of step-by-step analysis of potential boot problems

Setup

This lab requires a working computer running Windows 9x.

Process

1. You are first going to generate a POST error by removing the RAM and then booting your computer.

   a. Using proper ESD procedures, take the case off of your system unit and carefully remove all of the RAM.

   b. Turn your system on. You should now get a POST error of staccato, repetitive beeps. These beeps indicate that your system has no working RAM.

   c. Turn your system off.

   d. Carefully replace your RAM. Remember to follow proper ESD procedures.

   e. Boot your system to make sure that the RAM was replaced correctly and that it tallies up to the same amount as before you performed this procedure.

   f. Turn your system off again.

2. Now let's try for a different POST error by taking the video card out of your system.

→ **Note**

On rare occasions, some versions of Windows combined with certain video cards do not play well with this scenario. Windows might not recognize the video card properly when you reinsert the card or it might not automatically locate proper drivers. Use a test machine for this step if possible. If you need to use your primary machine, have a copy of the current video card drivers handy just in case.

a. First, remove the cable that connects the monitor to your video card.

b. Next, remove the screw at the top of the flange that holds the card securely in the case.

In systems that have the video card built into the motherboard, you will not be able to remove it.

c. Using proper ESD procedures, carefully but firmly grab the card by the sides and pull it out of its slot.

It may be difficult to remove at first—be gentle but persistent.

d. Once the card is removed, make sure to hold it like you would an expensive photograph, by its edges.

e. Look at the card. Can you see a ROM chip on your video card, similar to the one on your motherboard? (This isn't part of the POST exercise—just an opportunity to look at a video card!)

f. With the card out, turn your system back on.

There's no guarantee, but you *should* get an error beep code telling you that the video card is missing. (If you don't get this error, at least you got some practice removing a card from your system!)

g. Turn your system off and, using proper ESD procedures, return the card to its slot.

Make sure that the card is seated firmly by pressing down on it with the heel of your hand. Replace the screw in the flange. Always use a screw to hold expansion cards in place.

h. Reattach your monitor cable.

i. Turn your system on to make sure everything is working correctly.

j. Replace the case to your system unit.

3. Now you're going to leave hardware for a moment and take a look at how the boot process works.

a. To begin, boot (or reboot) your system.

b. When your system starts to run either DOS or Windows, press F8.

   If you interrupted a DOS boot, you have the option to select a step-by-step confirmation; if you interrupted a Windows 9x boot, it will bring up a menu with several options.

   If DOS or Windows starts, the system didn't receive your F8 instruction (you only have a brief window of time in which to press the correct key). Just reboot and try again.

c. Go step by step through the boot process, watching the system execute commands.

   DOS step-by-step

   1) If you are doing the DOS step-by-step confirmation, you will be given the option to run each line of your CONFIG.SYS file and your AUTOEXEC.BAT one by one or to skip any line you don't want to execute.

   2) Enter **Y** to run a line, or **N** not to run a line. If you type **N**, the system behaves as if that line is not in the file and simply skips it and moves on to the next one.

   3) You should not skip a line unless you have a specific reason, because it skips some part of the boot process that may be necessary.

   CONFIG.SYS

   Here are some lines from a CONFIG.SYS file with brief descriptions about what they do:

   DOS=HIGH   Moves part of your DOS kernel to the High Memory Area

   DOS=UMB   Prepares the Upper Memory Block in Reserved Memory for use

   Device=c:\windows\himem.sys   Enables the system to access Extended Memory

   Device=c:\windows\emm386.exe ram   Enables the system to use some of the Extended Memory as Expanded Memory

   Devicehigh=c:\cdrom\oakcdrom.sys /d:mscd000   This loads the driver for the CD-ROM in the UMB and names the device MSCD000

AUTOEXEC.BAT

Here are some typical lines from an AUTOEXEC.BAT file, with brief descriptions:

LH c:\windows\Mouse.com   Loads the driver for your system's mouse in the UMB.

LH c:\windows\mscdex.exe /d:mscd000   Assigns a drive letter to the device MSCD000 (see the last CONFIG.SYS instruction listed previously)

When you go through this process, you can see what your system is doing during the boot process. Remember that the lines listed previously are only examples. You should not expect every system to show you the same ones. In fact, most systems won't. Every system will be unique in the drivers it loads for CD-ROMs, sound cards, network interface cards, and so on.

Windows step-by-step

1)   If you press F8 to interrupt the boot process on a Windows 9x system, you will get a menu with several options.

2)   Select the option that enables you to perform a step-by-step confirmation.

3)   Run through a step-by-step process of loading up your system's GUI.

As you go through the step-by-step process, make a note of which drivers are being loaded and in which order.

You may see some of the lines mentioned previously in the DOS section if your system has CONFIG.SYS and AUTOEXEC.BAT files.

The first few times that you go through this step-by-step boot process, you may feel a bit overwhelmed, but persist—if you go through it a few times and take notes, you should soon feel comfortable using this excellent tool.

✔ **Tech Note**

The step-by-step boot process is one of the most useful troubleshooting techniques available to PC technicians. When devices do not work or a system locks up, performing the step-by-step procedure will frequently locate the culprit(s). If a system is locking up on boot, run through the step-by-step process answering "Yes" until the system locks up. Then reboot your system and answer "Yes" again until you reach the offending line again. At that line, respond with a "No" and see if you can continue successfully through the rest of the boot process.

Lab 4.3: Motherboard Layout, Installation, and Manuals

Objective

In this lab, you will become familiar with different motherboard layouts, practice removing and installing a motherboard, and learn about motherboard manuals. At the end of this lab, you should

- Recognize different motherboard form factors and the different parts of a motherboard

- Know how to install a motherboard safely and correctly

- Know how to get and use a motherboard manual

Setup

This lab requires at least one working computer. As usual, if you have access to more than one system, take advantage of it.

✖ **Warning**

Because this lab involves thoroughly dismantling the insides of a system with the attendant risk of ESD damage and overall potential for difficulties and delays, do not perform this lab with a computer that you can't afford to have out of commission.

Process

1. Open up your computer and take a good look at the motherboard.

    a. Do you have an AT or ATX motherboard? Here's what to look for:

        AT form factor

        - P8 and P9 power connections

        - 5-pin DIN keyboard connection

        - PC speaker connection

        - Turbo LED connection

- Hard drive activity LED connection

- Reset connection

- Keylock connection

ATX form factor

- P1 power connection

- PS2 keyboard connection

- PC Speaker connection

- "Soft" power connection

- Turbo LED connection

- Hard drive activity LED connection

- Reset connection

- Keylock connection

b. Compare your motherboard to the ones in Figures 4-5 and 4-6. If you have the option, open up several other computers and look at their motherboards.

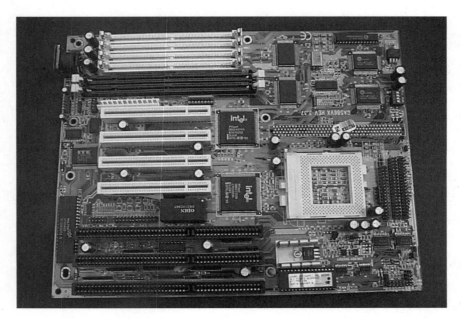

FIGURE 4-5 AT motherboard

Figure 4-6 ATX motherboard

c. How many expansion slots are there on your motherboard? _____

What types are they? _____

d. Find the following connections on your motherboard:

Floppy drive cable (note the location of the red stripe on the cable)

Hard drive cables (again, note the location of the red stripe on the cable)

CD-ROM (again, find the stripe)

e. What type of battery is on the motherboard? _____

f. Examine how the motherboard is held in the case. Motherboards mount to the case with small connectors called *standouts* that slide into keyed slots or screw into the bottom of the case. Screws then go into the standouts to hold the motherboard in place.

Find the screws. How many are there? _____

Find the plastic standouts. How many are there? _____

2. Now it's time to try removing and installing your motherboard. One more time, remember to use...that's right, proper ESD procedures!

   a. First, disconnect all cables and wires from the motherboard, noting where each one goes and its proper orientation.

   b. Next, remove the screws that hold the motherboard in place.

      Make sure that you store the screws and/or standouts in a tube or other safe place.

      Make sure that you don't misplace the cardboard washers for the screws. These not only provide insulation, but they also keep you from tightening the screws down hard enough to crack the motherboard.

   c. Carefully remove the motherboard from the case.

   ✖ **Warning**

   Remember to handle the motherboard as you should any printed circuit board: by the edges, as if it were a precious photograph.

   d. With the motherboard out of the case, look at the wires, or *traces*, running all over the surfaces of the board, top and bottom. These wires are the external data bus and the address bus. Can you tell which is which? Neither can I!

   e. Look for charts and numbers silk-screened onto the surface. You should be able to answer the following questions.

      What are the settings for the motherboard speed? _____

      What are the settings for the CPU timings? _____

      What are the settings for the CPU voltages? _____

   f. Try to find the name of the motherboard maker and the model number.

      Record this information: _____

      You can use this information to search the Internet for your motherboard manual if you cannot find it.

   g. After inspecting the motherboard, get some compressed air and clean it up. While you're at it, get the dust out of the case as well. Remember your ESD procedures.

h. Carefully put the motherboard back in the case, making sure your system is unplugged.

    1) Put all the screws and washers back where they belong.

    2) Connect all of the wires from the case to the motherboard.

    3) Make sure if you have an ATX motherboard that you have the soft power on.

    4) Properly orient (look for the stripe) and reconnect the cables for the hard drives and floppy drives.

i. Double-check everything you just did—*seriously*, double-check everything you just did—and then turn your system back on to verify that it is working properly.

3. Now that you have seen how the motherboard manual can come in handy, let's take a closer look at it.

a. Find the manual for your particular motherboard.

It's probably in the closet or your filing cabinet somewhere—look around.

Can't find it? Go online and search the Internet using that number off the motherboard you found in the last exercise.

b. Once you have a copy of the manual, open it and search for the treasures within.

Find out how to set the CPU speed. _____

Find out the minimum and maximum clock ratios. _____

Which of the following ways can you use to set the CPU speed and clock ratio on your motherboard?

    Jumpers_____

    DIP switches _____

    CMOS _____

Find out the minimum and maximum system speeds. _____

How do you set the system speed?

    Jumpers_____

    DIP switches _____

    CMOS _____

Find out where on the motherboard the following are connected:

PC speaker   _____

Reset switch _____

Power LED   _____

Hard drive activity LED   _____

Soft power wire (ATX only)   _____

CPU fan   _____

Find in the manual what the orientation is for the following:

Primary IDE connection   _____

Secondary IDE connection   _____

Floppy drive connection   _____

What does the manual mention about the following?

Serial port(s)_____

Parallel port _____

What are the minimum and maximum amounts of RAM your system will support? _____

What type of chipset do you have on your motherboard?   _____

How do you enter setup, according to the manual?_____

_____

What does the manual tell you about the control keys you use in the CMOS setup?

_____

How much detail does the manual give you about the various CMOS screens and what information they require? _____

Does the manual explain how to clear CMOS settings?   _____

Do you think this manual will come in handy again? (Yes!)   _____

Chapter 5

Expansion Bus

Your PC's expansion slots give you tremendous configuration flexibility when you add devices to your PC. Expansion slots provide a standardized interface for installing new devices. Many plug-and-play (PnP) devices today have some rather nasty habits and don't work properly. Understanding how motherboards and the expansion slots soldered to them work together in order to enable a sound card or modem to run properly is absolutely vital. In the following labs you'll look at expansion slots, install and remove expansion cards, and do some work with those pesky yet essential I/O addresses and IRQs.

Lab 5.1: Expansion Slots

Objective

In this lab, you will become familiar with the different types of expansion bus slots. At the end of this lab, you should

- Be able to find and identify the expansion bus slots on any motherboard

- Know the basic features of the different types of expansion bus slots

Setup

This lab requires at least one working computer running Windows 9x with cards installed in the expansion slots on the motherboard. As usual, if you have access to more than one system, take advantage of it.

Process

In Chapter 4's labs, you looked at the expansion slots on your motherboard. Now you need to find out what types of slots those are.

1. You should be able to identify different types of expansion slots on sight. Following are the basic features of the most important expansion slots.

   a. Industry Standard Architecture (ISA) slots

      - About 5 inches long

      - Black

      - Offset from edge of motherboard about ½ inch

      - ISA slots have two parts:

      8-bit

      - About 3 inches long

      - Metal connections on the inside

      16-bit

      - 1½ inches long

      - Metal connections on the inside

- Have a slight gap of about ¼ inch between the 8-bit and 16-bit portions of the ISA slot

- Original 8-bit ISA slots came out with the 8088s

- 16-bit ISA slots came out with the 286s

- 16-bit ISA slots are still on Pentium systems

b. Video Electronic Standards Association (VESA) slots

- Parasitic (function as an addition to 16-bit ISA slots)

- About 2 inches long

- Brown

- Capable of 32-bit data transfers

- Lasted through the 386 and 486 series of CPUs

c. Peripheral Component Interconnect (PCI) slots

- Most prevalent slots on motherboards today

- About 3 inches long

- White

- Offset from the edge of the motherboard about 1 inch

- PCI slots have metal connections on the inside

- Have a gap about 2½ inches down (away from the closest edge of the motherboard)

- Gave rise to plug-and-play

d. Accelerated Graphics Port (AGP) slot

- Used strictly for video cards

- 1 single slot per motherboard

- About 2¾ inches long

- Brown

- Offset from edge of motherboard about 2 inches

- AGP slots have metal connections on the inside

- Have a gap ¾ inch down (away from the closest edge of the motherboard)

2. Open your case and check out the expansion slots on the motherboard. Note how many ISA, PCI, and AGP slots your motherboard has.

   ISA   _____

   PCI   _____

   AGP   _____

3. How many ISA cards do you have on your system? How many PCI cards? What are they? Is there a card in the AGP slot? If not, what type of video card do you have?

   ISA cards   _____

   PCI cards   _____

   Video card   _____

4. Identify the expansion bus slots in Figure 5-1.

   A   _____

   B   _____

   C   _____

   D   _____

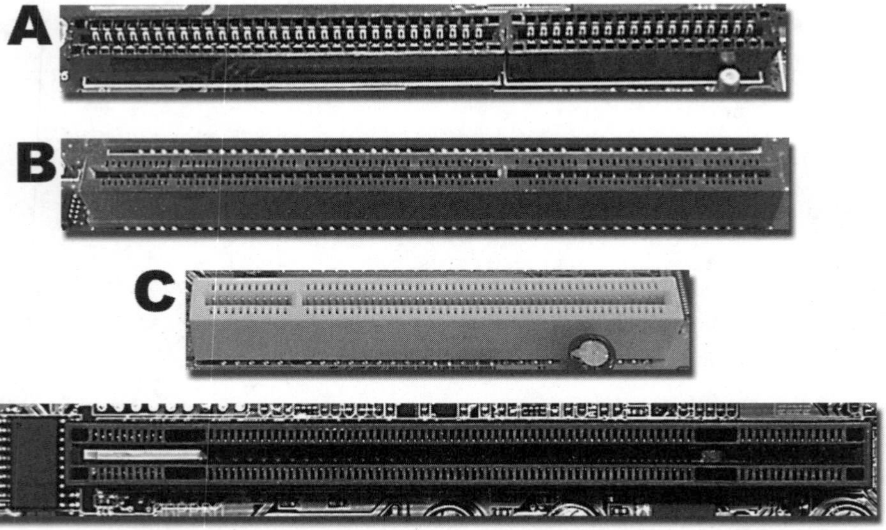

FIGURE 5-1 Expansion bus slots

Lab 5.2: I/O Addresses and IRQs

Objective

In this lab, you will reinforce your knowledge of I/O addresses and IRQs. At the end of this lab, you should

- Know the basic COM and LPT settings you need for the A+ exam
- Know how to use Device Manager to find out what I/O addresses are in use
- Know the rules of IRQ addressing and the default address assignments

Setup

This lab requires at least one working computer running Windows 9x with cards installed in the expansion slots on the motherboard. As usual, if you have access to more than one system, take advantage of it.

Process

1. Investigate the I/O addresses required by your expansion cards.

   a. Go into Device Manager and double-click the Computer icon. The Computer Properties window opens.

   b. Select the Input/Output (I/O) radio button to review the list of devices and their I/O addresses.

2. Study and memorize the COM and LPT settings in Table 5-1.

Port	I/O Address	IRQ
COM1	3F8	4
COM2	2F8	3
LPT1	378	7
LPT2	278	5

Table 5-1 COM and LPT Assignments

If you're studying with a partner, quiz him or her on the settings, and then have your partner quiz you.

Not only are these settings on the A+ exam, but they are also good real-world stuff to know.

3. List (from memory if possible) the three basic rules of I/O addresses.

_____

_____

_____

4. Review Table 5-2, and then cover it up and see if you can answer the following questions.

IRQ	Default Function
IRQ 0	System timer
IRQ 1	Keyboard
IRQ 2/9	Open for use
IRQ 3	Default COM2, COM4
IRQ 4	Default COM1, COM3
IRQ 5	LPT2
IRQ 6	Floppy drive
IRQ 7	LPT1
IRQ 8	Real-time clock
IRQ 10	Open for use
IRQ 11	Open for use
IRQ 12	Open for use
IRQ 13	Math-coprocessor
IRQ 14	Primary hard drive controller
IRQ 15	Secondary hard drive controller

TABLE 5-2 IRQ Assignments

Which IRQs are by default open for use? _____

Which IRQ is by default assigned to LPT1? _____

Which IRQ is by default assigned to the floppy drive? _____

Which IRQ is by default assigned to the primary hard drive controller? _____

Which IRQs are by default assigned to

    COM1   _____

    COM2   _____

    COM3   _____

    COM4   _____

5. Now you're going to do something a bit different as a test: hex/binary conversions. Hex and binary can be a little tricky, but converting them is a good skill for a PC tech to master—"real" techs can talk hex. The conversions are not tested on the A+ exams, but you will use them all the time in real life.

  a. Try writing down some binary and hex numbers at random and then try to convert them.

    For example:

      What is 1010 in hex? _____

      What is 1110 1100 in hex?_____

      What is D3F4 in binary? _____

      What is 02CB in binary? _____

    Now you try.

      Binary: _____ Hex: _____

      Binary: _____ Hex: _____

      Binary: _____ Hex: _____

      Hex: _____ Binary: _____

      Hex: _____ Binary: _____

      Hex: _____ Binary: _____

Lab 5.3: Expansion Card Installation and Removal

Objective

In this lab, you will practice removing and installing expansion cards. At the end of this lab, you should

- Recognize the major types of expansion cards found in a standard system
- Be able to install expansion cards in a system correctly and safely
- Be able to remove expansion cards from a system correctly and safely

Setup

This lab requires at least one working computer with expansion cards installed in the expansion slots on the motherboard. As usual, if you have access to more than one system, take advantage of it.

Process

1. First let's find out what you have installed in your system.

    a. Using proper ESD procedures, take the case off of your system unit.

    b. Determine how many expansion cards you have installed in your system. _____

    What type of cards are they?

    ISA? _____

    PCI? _____

    AGP? _____

    Are all of the expansion cards held down by screws?

    If not, remedy this immediately.

Try to determine the functions of these cards. See if you can you locate the following cards:

Video_____

Modem _____

Sound _____

Network interface _____

Others _____

2. Next, remove the cards from your system. Remember to follow ESD procedures.

   a. Take the retaining screw out and store it safely. Notice that this is a large-threaded screw similar to the ones that might hold the case on your system unit.

   b. Taking hold of a card by its edges, carefully and firmly pull it out of its slot. Before you remove it, make a mental note of which slot the card is in so you can return it to its original position.

   These cards can be difficult to remove. If a card seems stuck, try rocking it back and forth (from front to back, not side to side). Pull the card straight out of the slot upward. Use the "precious photograph" technique: Hold the card only by the edges and the flange (the silver bar that connects to the case).

3. Store expansion cards in an electrostatic bag for safekeeping.

4. Examine each of the cards you removed from your system.

   a. Do any of the cards have ROM on them?

   Is there a label or markings on this ROM?

   Record any pertinent information:

   _____

   _____

   _____

b.   Take a look at some of the chips on the expansion cards.

Do any of them have writing or labels on them?

Can you identify the manufacturers of the cards?

Are there any revision numbers or codes on the cards?

Record any pertinent information:

_____

_____

_____

c.   Are there jumpers or DIP switches on any of the cards?

How are they set?

Can you locate a "key" that shows you how to set the jumpers or DIP switches?

Record any pertinent information:

_____

_____

_____

5. Put the expansion cards that you removed back into your system.

a.   Take a card and position it perpendicular to the slot where it is to go. Make sure that the flange is toward the case.

b.   Holding the flange with one hand, place the heel of your hand over the card and firmly push the card into the expansion slot.

Some cards seem to have a mind of their own at this point and don't want to go in. Try this process:

1)   Tilt the card at about 20 degrees, flange end up.

2) Slowly place the other end of the card into the slot.

3) Roll the card into the slot by pushing the flange down to the case.

4) Make sure that the card stays perpendicular to the motherboard. Do not try to put a card in at a sideways angle; this could result in bent metal connectors in the expansion slot, possibly creating bad connections between the slot and the card.

c. Once the card is in the slot and the flange is flush with the case, replace the screw to hold the card in place.

6. Try to identify and find the features of the expansion card in Figure 5-2.

What type of card is it? _____

What type of expansion slot does it need?_____

Who is the maker of this card? _____

How many RAM chips do you see on this card? _____

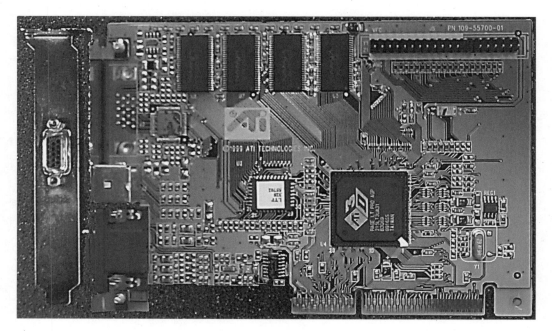

FIGURE 5-2 Mystery expansion card

Chapter 6
Power Supplies

The term *power supply* is a bit of a misnomer: The power supply does not supply power to your PC at all. After all, the electricity that powers your PC comes out of a wall socket and ultimately from a power company. Your PC uses DC voltage, but local power companies supply only AC voltage. Some conversion process must take place in order for the PC to function. The power supply in a PC actually acts as a step-down transformer, converting high-voltage AC, or alternating current (115 volts in the United States), into 5-, 12-, and 3.3-volt DC, or direct current. The PC uses the 12-volt current to power motors on devices such as hard drives and CD-ROM drives and the 5-volt and 3.3-volt currents for support of onboard electronics. Two types of power supplies make up over 99 percent of all power supplies installed in personal computers: AT and ATX. Even though AT form factor computers are fading away, their huge installed base requires you to recognize and understand the AT power supply. Most important, the A+ exam assumes that you have a solid understanding of both the AT and the ATX power supplies. In this chapter, you'll first practice the procedures for dealing with the "soft" power on ATX systems. Then you'll practice an important PC tech skill: the use of a multimeter.

> **→ Note**
>
> The A+ Core Hardware exam really shows its U.S. roots in the area of electrical power. Watch out for power questions that discuss U.S. power standards—especially ones related to household current and outlet plug design.

Lab 6.1: Soft Power

Objective

In this lab, you will become familiar with the requirements of working with soft power. At the end of this lab, you should

- Know the proper procedures for working on a soft power (ATX) system

Setup

This lab requires an ATX computer with a working power supply installed.

Process

1. If you are using an ATX system, you have soft power. Working with soft power requires a PC tech to take a few extra precautions. First, using proper ESD procedures, open your case and locate the power supply and the power switch (which is usually a button) on the outside front of the case.

2. A soft power configuration includes a wire running directly from the power switch on the front of the case to the motherboard (see Figure 6-1). Locate this wire and trace it from the power switch to the motherboard.

   a. Consult your motherboard's manual to find out where the soft power connector should be attached. The markings for attachment should also be clearly indicated on the motherboard, as shown in Figure 6-2.

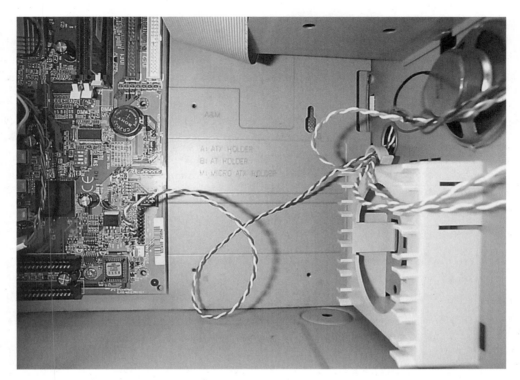

Figure 6-1 Soft power wire

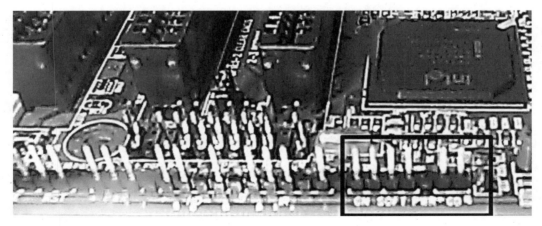

Figure 6-2 Soft power pins are labeled

When this wire is attached, it enables you to turn the system on and off through the motherboard. This means that there is always a *slight flow of electricity* through the motherboard. Therefore, if you are going connect or disconnect a component to your system, proper ESD procedures demand that you first unplug the system from the wall.

b.   If you cannot find where the soft power attaches to the motherboard, use a screwdriver to touch pairs of pins in the pins/jumpers area of the motherboard while the system is plugged in, as shown in Figure 6-3. When you place the metal end of the screwdriver between a pair of pins so it touches both of them, you form a closed circuit just like the connector would.

When you make a connection between the correct pair of pins, your system should start.

The CPU fan (as long as it's plugged in, naturally) will indicate when you hit the correct combination; the fan will spin as soon as electricity flows completely through the board.

Once you find the correct pair of pins, be sure to note where they are so that you can connect the soft power wire to the correct pair of pins.

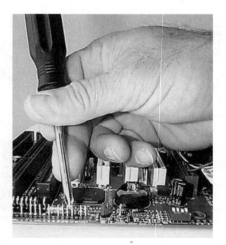

FIGURE 6-3 Finding the correct pair of pins for the soft power wire

3. Unplug your system from the wall. Hold on to your system case as you unplug the power cord to ensure that you and the system have the same electrical potential.

4. The end of the soft power wire not attached to the motherboard goes directly to the On/Off switch on the front of your case. Even when this On/Off switch is set to Off, some electricity is running to the motherboard. To be safe, you must unplug your system from the AC power source.

   Check the back of the system case where the power supply shows through. Some power supplies have a toggle On/Off switch on the back of the unit. Turning this switch to Off will prevent any power from reaching the motherboard.

   Nevertheless, play it safe: *Always* unplug a soft power system from the wall.

Lab 6.2: Multimeter Mastery

Objective

In this lab, you will practice using a multimeter to test the current in various parts of the power system. At the end of this lab, you should

- Know how to test a wall socket
- Know how to test the motherboard power connectors
- Know how to test a Molex connector

Setup

This lab requires a computer you can open and conduct tests on. As usual, if you have access to more than one system, take advantage of it.

Process

1. Get your trusty multimeter and head over to a wall socket to measure the AC. First, examine the wall socket closely.

   a. Notice that the typical wall socket has three openings, as shown in Figure 6-4.

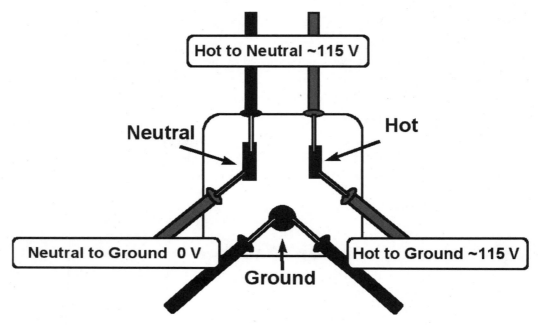

Figure 6-4 Multimeter probe locations when testing AC socket

Two rectangular slots that are parallel to each other:

- One a little longer (neutral)
- One a little shorter (hot)

One round opening (ground)

b.   Set your multimeter to AC voltage. Do not proceed until you are sure you have done this correctly (see Figure 6-5).

c.   First you will measure the current in the hot to ground circuit.

1)   Take the black probe and place it in the ground opening of the socket. Make sure you have good contact in the receptacle.

2)   Take the red probe and place it in the hot opening. Don't worry—as long as you have insulation on the probes, you'll be fine. Make sure you have good contact in the receptacle.

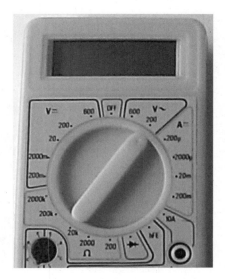

Figure 6-5 Multimeter set to test AC voltage

3) Move the probes around until you get a good reading for the AC current.

   With common AC, the electrical power is about 115 volts. You may get a variance of plus or minus 10 percent.

4) Record your readings: _____

d. Next you will measure the current in the hot to neutral circuit.

   1) Take the black probe and place it in the neutral opening of the socket. Make sure you have good contact in the receptacle.

   2) Take the red probe and place it in the hot opening. Don't worry—as long as you have insulation on the probes, you'll be fine. Make sure you have good contact in the receptacle.

   3) Move the probes around until you get a good reading for the AC current.

      With common AC, the electrical power is about 115 volts. You may get a variance of plus or minus 10 percent.

   4) Record your readings: _____

e. Next you will measure the current in the neutral to ground circuit.

1) Take the black probe and place it in the ground opening of the socket. Make sure you have good contact in the receptacle.

2) Take the red probe and place it in the neutral opening. Don't worry—as long as you have insulation on the probes, you'll be fine. Make sure you have good contact in the receptacle.

3) Move the probes around until you get a good reading for the AC current. You should get a reading of 0 volts.

4) Record your readings: _____

f. Go to another outlet in the same building and repeat the previous steps. Are the readings similar?

2. Now head back over to your computer so you can measure the DC power circuits inside your system.

a. Using proper ESD techniques, take the cover off of your system unit.

b. Set your multimeter to DC so that you can measure the voltages produced by your system's power supply. Figure 6-6 shows a multimeter set to test DC current.

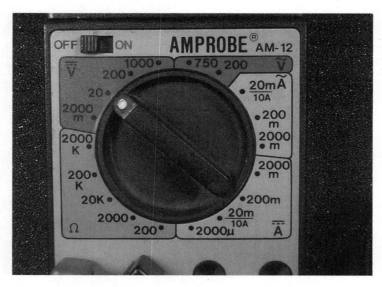

FIGURE 6-6 Multimeter set to a 20-volt DC range

✖ **Warning**

The power supply must *always* have something connected to the DC side—a *load* in electrician-speak—when it is plugged into the wall to allow the direct current to flow. Failure to provide a load will *destroy* your power supply.

✔ **Tech Note**

If you are going to test DC power, your system must be *turned on*. It's a little thing, I know, but in order to have DC power to test, the system must be on.

c.   Find the power connection from the power supply to the motherboard. Determine which type of power connector your system has: P8/P9 (Figure 6-7) or P1 (Figure 6-8).

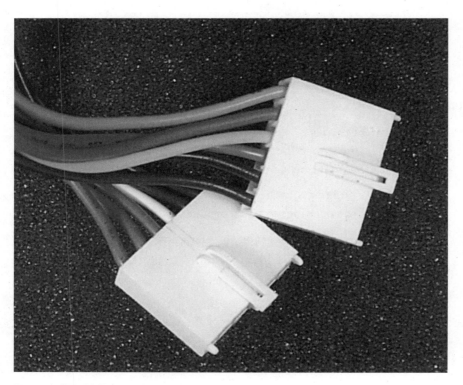

FIGURE 6-7 P8/P9 connector

FIGURE 6-8 P1 connector

d.   If you have an AT system (P8/P9 connector), test the voltage of the connector as follows.

1)   Place the end of the black probe into one of the areas where a black wire (ground) goes into either the P8 or P9 connector. Make sure that you get good contact with the metal inside the opening.

2)   Starting at one end (usually the orange wire), place the red probe down into another one of the openings to make contact with the metal.

3)   Record the readings that you get as you work down through all the wires.

You may have to jiggle the probes a little to make sure you get good contact. If the numbers on the multimeter keep tallying higher and higher, your power supply is probably not on—you were warned about that earlier.

You should find that most of the voltages are positive, but a few will give you negative readings. Remember, "DC" stands for direct current—it goes in one side and out the other.

e. If you have an ATX system (P1 connector), test the voltage of the connector as follows.

1) Place the end of the black probe into one of the openings where a black wire (ground) is connected. Make sure that you have contact with the metal inside the opening.

2) Place the end of the red probe into any of the other openings. Make sure that you have contact with the metal inside the opening.

3) Record the readings that you get as you work down through all the wires.

You may have to jiggle the probes a little to make sure you have good contact. If the numbers on the multimeter keep tallying higher and higher, your power supply is probably not on—you were warned about this earlier.

Again, you should find that most of the voltages are positive, but a few will give you a negative reading.

f. Now let's test a Molex connection. When you test a Molex connection, it is best if it is *not* connected to a device.

✖ Warning

Remember, you still need to have a load on the power supply, so something else had better be connected (usually the motherboard).

1) Take the end of the black probe and place it in the round hole at the end of the Molex associated with a black wire.

2) Take the end of the red probe and place it in the round hole at the end of the Molex associated with either the red or yellow wire.

3) Make sure you have a good connection—you may have to jiggle the probes a little.

4) Record your findings:

_____

5) Now do the other wire.

6) Record your findings:

_____

3. Congratulate yourself! You are now a multimeter professional.

Chapter 7
Floppy Drives

Floppy drives enjoy the unique distinction of being the only components of a modern PC to contain basically the same technology as the original IBM PC. Hard to believe, but when the first PCs came out, the entire permanent storage system consisted of a single floppy drive! Since those early days, there have been huge advances in portable storage technology, yet the PC industry continues to use floppy drives despite their ancient technology and tiny capacities. If the PC industry—and that includes software makers, especially Microsoft—ever decides on a single standard for a floppy drive replacement that ensures broad compatibility, the venerable floppy drive will disappear. But until that day (which, by the way, is nowhere in sight), we will continue to use floppy drives. And while that remains the case, the A+ exams will continue to expect you to know how to deal with them.

Lab 7.1: Configuring a Floppy Drive

Objective

In this lab, you will use the CMOS setup program to configure a floppy drive. At the end of this lab, you should

- Be able to locate the CMOS setup screen for configuring floppy drives
- Know the proper settings for configuring a floppy drive

Setup

This lab requires at least one working computer with a floppy drive installed.

Process

1. Go into CMOS by pressing the appropriate keystroke combinations (which you should have recorded in the lab for Chapter 4) while your system is booting.

   Having previously browsed through your version of CMOS, you should be able to go to the area where you can set up the type of floppy drive that your system is using. If you cannot remember where that is, browse.

→ **Note**

   It is usually in the Standard CMOS Setup screen, shown in Figure 7-1.

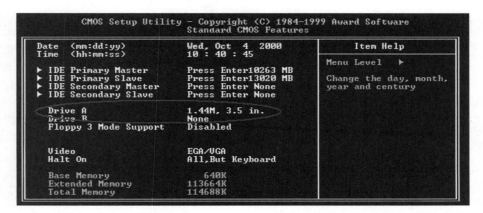

FIGURE 7-1 Standard CMOS Setup screen

2. Determine how many floppy drives you have set up on your system, according to CMOS. _____

3. Using the control features, determine how many different types of floppy drives can be set up on your system.

   Do you have a None setting? _____

   How many different types of 5-1/4-inch drives can be set up? _____

   How many different types of 3-1/2-inch drives can be set up? _____

   What, if any, other types of drives can be set up? _____

4. Write down the Type setting of the floppy drive on your system. _____

5. Now change the Type setting of the floppy drive to None.

   (Don't worry, you'll reset this in the next lab.)

6. Look around in other areas of CMOS for a Swap Floppy Device option.

   What heading is that option found under?_____

7. Do you have an option in CMOS to disable the floppy drive controller? _____

   What heading is that option found under?_____

   How do you disable this setting?_____

   Do it! You will set it back (enable it) in the next lab.

✔ **Tech Note**

Disabling the floppy drive connector is a good way for a network administrator to prevent users from either taking information off of the network or introducing viruses into the network.

---

8. Exit CMOS correctly, making sure to save any changes you might have made.

Lab 7.2: Removing and Installing a Floppy Drive

Objective

In this lab, you will practice removing and installing a floppy drive. At the end of this lab, you should

- Be able to remove a floppy drive safely and correctly
- Be able to install a floppy drive safely and correctly

Setup

This lab requires at least one working computer with a floppy drive installed.

Process

1. First you are going to remove your floppy drive.

    a. Using proper ESD procedures, open your case and disconnect the floppy cable from the motherboard.

    1) Look and see where the orientation stripe is positioned, as shown in Figure 7-2.

    These cables can be quite firmly attached to the motherboard. Use the following procedure to remove one:

    Grab the connector, or as close to the connector as you can, and pull straight up firmly but gently. Sometimes a connector will start to grab on one side—make sure that you do not pull unevenly, or you will bend the pins on the motherboard.

    b. Look at the motherboard where the cable was attached.

    1) Examine the pins of the connections in that area of the motherboard.

    How many freestanding pins do you count? _____

    How many pins enclosed in plastic do you count? _____

    2) Look at the shape of the connection.

    Is it symmetrical or is one side "keyed"? _____

    3) Find #1 pin.

Figure 7-2 Orientation of floppy drive cable on motherboard

4) Find the 34th pin.

The 34th pin is the Drive Change Signal/Disk Change signal. It indicates whether or not your diskette has been switched. If this wire is broken or not connected, every disk will read as the initial disk in the system the first time it's used during a session.

✔ **Tech Note**

If your floppy drive behaves strangely, check to make sure that the 34th pin is registering.

c.   Disconnect the floppy cable from the floppy drive.

   1)   Make sure that you note the location of the orientation stripe before you disconnect the cable.

   _____

   2)   Look at the shape of the connection to the floppy drive.

   Is the connection symmetrical or is one side keyed? That is, does the ribbon cable connector have a small ridge on one side to prevent incorrect insertion? _____

   How many connectors does the cable have? _____

d.   Disconnect the mini-connector from the floppy drive.

   1)   Try to find the platter on the floppy drive that corresponds with the square indentation on the mini-connector. (See Figure 7-3.)

   Did you feel or hear a "click" from the notch on that indentation?

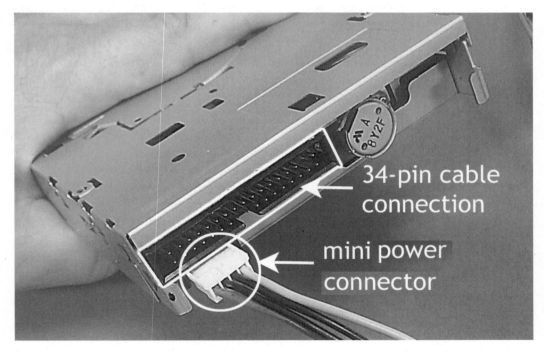

Figure 7-3 Back end of a floppy drive showing the motherboard and power connections

e. Remove the floppy drive from the case.

There are so many different ways that floppy drives are held in system cases that it would be impossible to list here all of the various carriers, caddies, stagnant bays, and so on that might be used to hold your floppy drive.

However, almost all floppy drives are secured to these carriers, caddies, and bays with the same type of screw: a finely threaded screw. The threads are narrower than the screws commonly used to secure expansion cards and hard drives.

There should be two screws in each side of the floppy drive for support.

2. Now that you've removed the floppy drive, let's inspect it.

a. Look at the area where the cable connects.

Again, is this area keyed or notched?

Try to find the indicator of which is the #1 pin.

What is it? _____

On which side of the connector does the red orientation stripe of the cable go?

Inside _____ Outside _____

How many physical pins are there? _____

How many spots for pins are there? _____

b. Look at the area where the power is attached.

How many pins are there? _____

Experiment to see if you can insert the power connector incorrectly.

Can you connect it upside down? _____

Can you connect it without covering every pin? _____

On which side of the mini-connector does the red wire go?

Inside _____Outside _____

3. Reinstall the floppy drive.

a. Place the floppy drive back into the bay from which you took it.

b. Using the small threaded screws, secure the floppy drive in the bay.

c.   Attach the mini-connector to the floppy drive to ensure that it has electricity to run.

d.   Attach the cable to the floppy drive and make sure that it is secure.

e.   Attach the cable to the motherboard. Make sure it is secure and that all the pins are covered.

   Without the guards around the floppy drive connector, it would be easy to

   • Miss an entire row of pins

   • Miss a set of pins

   • Put the floppy cable on backwards

f.   Once everything is back in place (the cover should still be off, as you might need to make adjustments), start the system and go into CMOS.

   Reset the CMOS settings you changed in Lab 7-1 (recall that you set Type to None and disabled the floppy drive controller) back to their original settings, then save your changes and exit.

g.   Make sure your system and the floppy drive are working properly, then turn off your system.

h.   Reverse the cable on either the floppy drive or the motherboard.

   By reverse, I mean change the direction of the orientation stripe on the connection. Do this on one side only!

i.   Turn your system on and look at the front of the floppy drive. The light indicating that the system is reading a disk should come on and stay on.

✔ Tech Note

A floppy drive light that never goes off is an indicator that the floppy drive cable is reversed in some fashion. This does not hurt the floppy drive; you just can't use it.

j.   Turn your system off and correct the cable orientation.

k.   Turn your system back on and make sure everything is working correctly.

Chapter 8

Hard Drives

Of all the hardware on a PC, none gets more attention—
or gives more anguish—than the hard drive. There's a good
reason for this: If the hard drive breaks, you lose data. As
we all know, when the data goes, you have to redo work or
restore data from backup—or worse. It's good to worry about
data, because data runs the office, maintains the payrolls,
and stores the e-mail. This level of concern is so strong that
even the most neophyte PC user is exposed to terms like
"backup," "defragment," and "scandisk"—even if they
don't put the concepts into practice! PC techs are expected
to deal with hard drives all the time, and the creators of
the A+ exam know this. These labs are designed to give
you the practical knowledge you need to install, format,
and configure these critical PC components.

Lab 8.1: Configuring a Hard Drive in CMOS

Objective

In this lab, you will use the CMOS setup program to configure a hard drive. At the end of this lab, you should

- Be able to locate the CMOS setup screen for configuring hard drives

- Know the proper settings for configuring a hard drive

Setup

This lab requires at least one working computer with a hard drive installed.

Process

1. Go into CMOS by pressing the appropriate keystroke combinations while your system is booting.

2. Go to the screen containing the geometries for the system's hard drive(s). Although it depends on your version of CMOS, you can usually find the geometries on the Standard CMOS Setup screen, as shown in Figure 8-1.

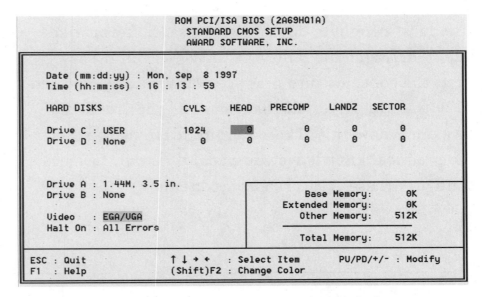

FIGURE 8-1 Drive geometries usually hang out in the Standard CMOS Setup screen

How many hard drives do you have set up on your system, according to CMOS? _____

Write down the settings for the drive(s)—you'll need them later.

_____

_____

Change the Hard Disk types on your system to None. This removes the hard drive's geometry from CMOS. (Don't worry, you will reset this later!) Make certain to set the drive to None for the purposes of this exercise, and not to Auto. You won't hurt anything if you set it to the latter, but the exercise will not work as planned.

3. Exit CMOS correctly, making sure to save any changes you might have made. Reboot normally.

What happened? _____

With most systems, the PC will go through the boot process and then stop when it can't find a bootable drive. It will then wait for you to insert a floppy disk.

4. Reboot the PC and return to CMOS. Go to the screen containing the geometries for the hard drives and replace the information you removed earlier. (Aren't you glad you wrote it down?)

5. Once you finish that, look for an option in CMOS to disable the hard drive controllers.

This option may look somewhat different depending on the version of CMOS you're using. Look for a menu option like one of these:

- Primary and Secondary IDE settings
- PCI Primary and Secondary IDE
- Onboard IDE settings

Under what heading did you find this option? _____

You can usually find it under Integrated Peripherals.

Can you figure out how to disable this setting? Do it! (Don't worry, you will set it back/enable it later.)

6. Exit CMOS correctly, making sure to save any changes you might have made.

7. Leaving the CMOS settings disabled and changed, reboot your system and see what happens.

Your system will look for a disk to boot from because you told it you had a hard drive when you reinserted the geometry settings, right? When the system isn't able to find a disk (because you disabled the controller), it will probably hang for a long period of time and then return a Primary Hard Drive Failure code or error message. Some systems try to recognize the fact that you have a hard drive regardless of the disabling of features, but this is very rare.

✔ **Tech Note**

Some systems will not let you disable the Primary and Secondary IDE controllers to begin with.

8. Reboot and go back into CMOS.

   a.   If your system has an option called something like "IDE HDD Auto Detection," choose it (see Figure 8-2).

```
                    ROM PCI/ISA BIOS (2A69HQ1A)
                        CMOS SETUP UTILITY
                      AWARD SOFTWARE, INC.
   ┌────────────────────────────────┬────────────────────────────────┐
   │  STANDARD CMOS SETUP            │  INTEGRATED PERIPHERALS         │
   │  BIOS FEATURES SETUP            │  SUPERVISOR PASSWORD            │
   │  CHIPSET FEATURES SETUP         │  USER PASSWORD                  │
   │  POWER MANAGEMENT SETUP         │  IDE HDD AUTO DETECTION         │
   │  PNP/PCI CONFIGURATION          │  HDD LOW LEVEL FORMAT           │
   │  LOAD BIOS DEFAULTS             │  SAVE & EXIT SETUP              │
   │  LOAD SETUP DEFAULTS            │  EXIT WITHOUT SAVING            │
   ├────────────────────────────────┴────────────────────────────────┤
   │  Esc : Quit                  ↑ ↓ → ←    : Select Item            │
   │  F10 : Save & Exit Setup     (Shift)F2 : Change Color            │
   └───────────────────────────────────────────────────────────────────┘
```

FIGURE 8-2 IDE HDD Auto Detection

The system should try to find your hard drive.

What happened? _____

If your system enabled you to disable the Primary and Secondary IDE controllers, autodetect should have come up empty handed.

Why? _____

9. It's time to show the power of autodetect, so reboot and go back into CMOS setup.

    a. If your system allowed you to disable the Primary and Secondary IDE controllers, reset them to enabled.

    b. Now run autodetect.

        The system should try to find your hard drive. If it succeeds, you should see two or three options for setting up your hard drive.

        List the options for your system:

        _____

        _____

        _____

    c. Select the top option, or the one that mentions LBA.

    d. If you have more than one hard drive, step through the subsequent menu options, again selecting the LBA option.

9. Exit CMOS correctly, making sure to save any changes you made.

Lab 8.2: FDISK

Objective

In this lab, you will practice formatting and partitioning a hard drive. At the end of this lab, you should

- Know how to set up a primary, active partition on a hard drive
- Know how to set up an extended partition and logical drives in that partition on a hard drive

Setup

This lab requires at least one working computer running Windows 98 with a second blank (that is, containing *no* data), unpartitioned hard drive installed.

✖ Warning

Doing this lab will destroy any data residing on the hard drive you use, so be completely sure there is nothing on it you can't live without!

Process

1. Boot your system using a Windows 98 boot disk.

   a. Select the "Start computer without CD-ROM support" option when prompted.

   b. When you get to the C: prompt, type in the command **FDISK** and press ENTER. (FDISK is a program that sets up partitions on a fixed disk.)

   c. If FDISK finds a hard drive on your system, it will ask you if you want to enable large disk support. Press the Y key (for yes) to accept, and the menu shown in Figure 8-3 should appear in response.

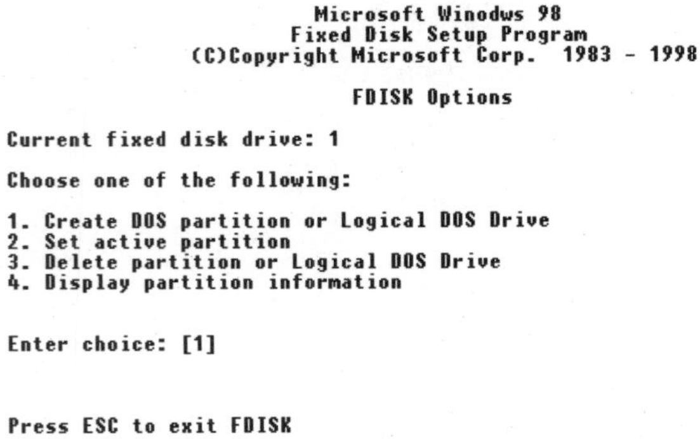

```
                        Microsoft Winodws 98
                      Fixed Disk Setup Program
              (C)Copyright Microsoft Corp.  1983 - 1998

                          FDISK Options

Current fixed disk drive: 1

Choose one of the following:

1. Create DOS partition or Logical DOS Drive
2. Set active partition
3. Delete partition or Logical DOS Drive
4. Display partition information


Enter choice: [1]


Press ESC to exit FDISK
```

FIGURE 8-3 FDISK Menu screen

This menu has four options:

1. Create DOS partition or Logical DOS Drive

2. Set active partition

3. Delete partition or Logical DOS Drive

4. Display partition information

At the bottom of the screen you should see the instruction to press ESC to exit FDISK. You can press ESC to go back to the previous screen as well.

d. Begin by selecting menu option 4. Display partition information to see if there are any partitions on this drive.

e. If there are partitions, you need to remove them. From the primary FDISK menu, select option 3 and then follow the screen instructions to delete any partitions. Note that you will lose *everything* on that drive, so make certain to back everything up *before* you trash the existing partitions! Once you've finished deleting partitions and have a clean drive, continue to the next step.

f. Okay, now that there are no partitions on the drive, let's add some. You'll want to make a primary partition first, so select the Create DOS Partition or Logical DOS Drive option (see Figure 8-4).

```
                    Create DOS Partition or Logical DOS Drive
        Current fixed disk drive: 1

        Choose one of the following:

        1. Create Primary DOS Partition
        2. Create Extended DOS Partition
        3. Create Logical DOS Drive(s) in the Extended DOS Partition



        Enter choice: [1]




        Press ESC to return to FDISK Options
```

FIGURE 8-4 FDISK Partition Menu screen

You should see a menu with three choices:

1. Create Primary DOS Partition

2. Create Extended DOS Partition

3. Create Logical DOS Drive(s) in the Extended DOS Partition

g. Select menu option 1. Create Primary DOS Partition.

FDISK will ask, "Do you want to use the entire drive as a Primary Partition and make it Active?" Well, yes, but no. You do want the primary partition to be active, but you do not want the entire drive to be one partition.

1) Press the N key and then ENTER to get to other options.

2) FDISK then makes the following request: "Enter the size of the drive in Megabytes or Percentage space." Use a percentage and enter **60%**. Do not forget the percent sign—otherwise, your primary partition will be only 60 megabytes!

Your screen should change to indicate that the C: drive is now 60 percent of your hard drive.

3) Press ESC once to return to the previous menu.

You should now be at the main menu screen again, with a warning flashing on the screen about not having an active partition. What option do you think you should select now?

h. If you said option 2, you're right! Select option 2. Set Active Partition, and when prompted, select the C: drive. You should now see an "A" (for "Active") in the Status field for the C: drive.

i. Now you need to assign the remaining 40 percent of the hard drive. Once again, select option 1. Create DOS Partition or Logical DOS Drive(s).

1) You should see the menu with the three partitioning choices again (see Figure 8-4). This time, select option 2. Create Extended DOS Partition.

FDISK will ask you how much of the drive you want this partition to occupy. Notice that FDISK is showing you how much of the drive is available for use. If you want less than this amount, you must tell FDISK.

2) In this case, however, you'll want to use the entire rest of the drive for the extended partition, so you can just press ENTER.

A screen should pop up showing that you have the C: drive as your primary partition, and that the rest of your hard drive is an extended partition.

3) Press ESC one time. A statement should appear saying that you have no "logical" drives. After a brief calculation, FDISK prompts you to enter the size logical drive you want. By default, the remaining disk space in megabytes is listed.

4) Type in **50%** and press ENTER. FDISK should show you at the top of the screen that a D: drive was created and its size. FDISK also displays that 50 percent of the extended partition is still available, and it asks how much of it you want for another logical drive.

5) To use the rest of it, press ENTER. Now at the top of the screen you should see an E: drive along with the D: drive, and their percentages should add up to 100 percent. You have now used all of your extended partition with logical drives (D: and E:).

6) Press ESC until you return to the main menu. Then select the Display Partition Information option. You will see information about the way your hard drive is partitioned.

7) Press ESC until you exit FDISK completely and then reboot your system. Changes made in FDISK are not accepted unless you exit the program completely and then reboot your system. Get used to it—that's the way it is!

Lab 8.3: Formatting a Hard Drive

Objective

In this lab, you will practice formatting a hard drive. At the end of this lab, you should

- Be able to format a hard drive correctly

Setup

This lab requires at least one working computer running Windows 98 with a second blank (that is, containing *no* data), unpartitioned hard drive installed.

> ✖ **Warning**
>
> Doing this lab will destroy any data residing on the hard drive you use, so be completely sure there is nothing on it you can't live without!

Process

1. Boot your system with the Windows 98 boot disk.

2. At the A: prompt, type the FORMAT command, as follows:

   FORMAT C:/s

   C: indicates the drive targeted for formatting.

   /s causes the system files to transfer to the boot record of the target drive.

   The system files are

   - IO.SYS

   - MSDOS.SYS

   - COMMAND.COM

   (You'll also likely see the file DRVSPACE.BIN—important for compressed drives, but not for most systems.)

   The system files only need to be on the active partition.

   The FORMAT command causes your system to do several things:

   - Lay out a grid on the hard drive for tracking where the data is located

   - Create a File Allocation Table to track the data

   - Give the drive a root directory

3. You will be told that if you format the drive you will lose data and you will be asked, "Are You Sure? Y/N." Press Y (for "yes") and then ENTER.

   The system will begin formatting the hard drive, and your screen will show the system's progress in percentages. Some drives will display a message stating that the system is "trying to recover allocation units" while the formatting is going on. This means that your hard drive has an area that is not reliable enough to use for data storage.

4. At the end of the formatting process, you will be asked to enter a Volume label. If you feel like giving the drive a name, go for it; otherwise, just press ENTER.

5. If you have a second drive to experiment on, repeat the FORMAT process, omitting /s because you only need one system drive (see Figure 8-5).

```
A:\>format C:/s

WARNING:  ALL DATA ON NON-REMOVABLE DISK
DRIVE C:  WILL BE LOST!
Proceed with Format  (Y/N)?y

Formatting  30709.65M
Format complete.
System transferred

Volume label (11 characters, ENTER for none)?

32,197,017,600 bytes total disk space
         262,144 bytes used by system
32,196,755,456 bytes available on disk

      491,520 bytes in each allocation unit.
      982,455 allocation units available on disk.

Volume Serial Number is 3166-11D9
```

FIGURE 8-5 FORMAT command

Lab 8.4: Removing and Reinstalling a Hard Drive

Objective

In this lab, you will practice removing and reinstalling a hard drive. At the end of this lab, you should

- Be able to remove a hard drive safely and correctly

- Be able to install a hard drive safely and correctly

Setup

This lab requires at least one working computer with a hard drive installed.

Process

1. Turn your system off and open the system case, following proper ESD procedures, of course!

2. Note the orientation of the cable(s) to the motherboard, and then unplug the ribbon cables that connect the motherboard to the IDE drives. Be careful but firm. Grasp the cables as close to the connector on the motherboard as possible and lift.

_____

3. Look at the IDE connections on the motherboard (see Figure 8-6).

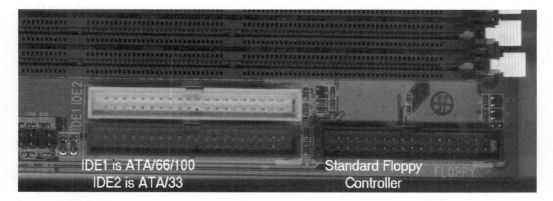

FIGURE 8-6 IDE connectors on a motherboard

Are they freestanding? _____ Or are they surrounded by plastic? _____

Are they keyed? _____

What color are they? _____

Look very closely at the motherboard and see if you can find writing on the board next to the IDE controllers that indicates the proper pin orientation.

Count the pins. How many are there? _____

Do you see any missing pins? _____

Look at the rest of the cable. Is it connected to anything else? _____

How many devices are there? 1 device _____ 2 devices _____

What types of devices (hard drive, CD-ROM) are hooked up to the Primary IDE or the IDE 1? _____

What types of devices are hooked up to the Secondary IDE or the IDE 2? _____

_____

4. Disconnect all of the devices from the IDE ribbon cables. But first note which device is connected to which cable and where the orientation stripe is located on each device.

_____

_____

5. Examine the IDE ribbon cable.

How many connections does it have for pins? _____

Are any of the holes on the cable connector filled in? _____

How many connectors does the ribbon cable have? _____

Where are the connectors on the cable? _____

6. Disconnect all of the IDE devices from the power supply.

✔ **Tech Note**

Molex plugs can be difficult to remove. There are little "bumps" on either side of the plug that will allow you to rock it back and forth to remove it.

---

7. Carefully remove the IDE drives from your system using proper ESD procedures.

Because of the great variety of cases, caddies, bays, slots, and so on, it's not possible to give detailed instructions on how to get these drives out of your particular system.

✔ **Tech Note**

Here are some good PC tech procedures to follow: Look carefully, think *before* you act, and don't force anything. Also, if you've got one, read the manual.

Remove the screws that are holding the drives in the bays and examine them closely. The screws for hard drives are of the large thread variety. CD-ROM drives, by comparison, use smaller threaded screws.

8.   Once you have the hard drive out of the system and in a static-free place, ground yourself, pick it up, and examine it carefully.

   a.   Note its dimensions. It should measure about $6 \times 3\frac{1}{2} \times 1$ inches. Some drives may be larger than this, measuring $6 \times 5\frac{1}{4} \times 1$ inches—these are known as "bigfoot" drives. Some drives are smaller, but they are used mostly in laptops.

   b.   Look at the largest surfaces of the drive (the top and bottom, as it were). One should be a printed circuit board with a ROM chip on it. The other should have a label listing some specs for the drive (see Figure 8-7), including (record the specs of your drive)

FIGURE 8-7 Specs on hard drive label

The geometries _____

How to set the jumpers (sometimes you even get a diagram) _____

Jumper Diagram

The maker and version of the drive _____

9.   Look at the "back" end of the drive (see Figure 8-8). You should see the IDE connection and the power connection right next to each other.

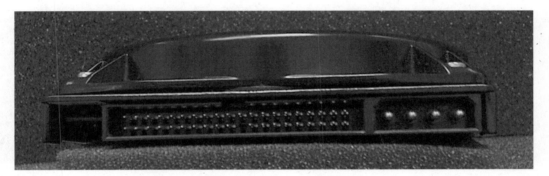

Figure 8-8 Connections on the "back" end of a hard drive

10.   Somewhere on the drive you should find the actual physical jumpers. Per the instructions on the label, these must be set for either:

   •   Master: the main drive on the IDE cable

   •   Slave: the subservient drive on the IDE cable

✔ **Tech Note**

The Master/Slave jumper settings *must* be correct for two drives to work on the same cable. This is a good place to start when troubleshooting a hard drive.

How are the jumpers set on this hard drive? (See Figure 8-9.) _____

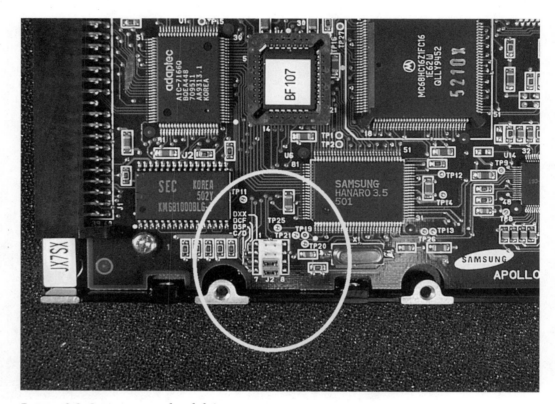

Figure 8-9 Jumpers on a hard drive

11. After you inspect the hard drive, reinstall it using a reverse version of the procedure you used to remove it, as follows:

a. Physically replace the drive.

b. Connect the power cable.

c. Connect the ribbon cable to the drive.

d. Connect the ribbon cable to the motherboard.

e. Turn on your system and auto-detect the drive.

Chapter 9

DOS

In the late 1970s, IBM began to search for a company that could provide them with an operating system (OS) for a new computer they were developing called the IBM Personal Computer, better known as the PC. They went to a tiny company that had invented a popular new programming language called BASIC and asked them to create an OS for the IBM PC. Although the young president's company had never written an OS, he brazenly said, "Sure!" That man was Bill Gates, and the tiny company was Microsoft. For a few thousand dollars, Gates bought a very primitive OS called QDOS (Quick-and-Dirty Operating System), and after making several minor changes, Microsoft released it as MS-DOS (MicroSoft Disk Operating System) version 1.1. Although primitive by today's standards, MS-DOS 1.1 performed all the necessary functions of an operating system. The last Microsoft version, MS-DOS 6.22, was released in 1994.

Although A+ Certification has dropped DOS from the examination domains, you should not assume that means you don't need to know DOS. The A+ Certification exams still assume you have a solid understanding of a large number of command-line programs such as FDISK and FORMAT. They also test you on DOS memory usage and configuring DOS programs in a Windows environment. Each command covered in these labs works in every version of Windows, and often offers a quicker way to accomplish a task than its graphical alternative. Further, the A+ exams test you on all of these commands.

Lab 9.1: DOS Filename and Directory Basics

Objective

Techs who grew up in a Windows world might find DOS files, filenames, and directory structures a bit less than intuitive. In this lab, you will reinforce your knowledge of DOS filename conventions and directory structures. At the end of this lab, you should

- Know the rules of 8.3 filenames and be able to recognize "illegal" filenames
- Be comfortable writing file pathnames using the DOS directory structure

Setup

All you need for this lab is your brain.

Process

1. First, let's review the logic and rules of the 8.3 naming system.

    - DOS manifests each program and piece of data as an individual file. Each file has a name, which is stored with the file on the drive.

    - Names are broken down into two parts: the filename and the extension. The filename can be no longer than eight characters. The extension, which is optional, can be up to three characters long.

    - No spaces or other "illegal" characters (/ \ [ ] | < > + = ; , * ?) can be used in the filename or extension.

    - The filename and extension are separated by a period, or *dot*. This naming system is known as the *eight dot three* (written "8.3") system.

2. Look at the following list of files. Circle those that *do not* follow the rules for 8.3 filenames:

MYST.EXE	WHY?WHYNOT.TXT	KIRK/SPOCK.DOC
THE.FORCE.MOV	OBI_WAN.COM	YES,PLEASE.EXE
[QUAKE]II.INI	LED ZEP.WAV	NY*GIANTS.BMP
CHAPTER17.WPD	SYSTEM.INI	hansolo.gif
X-FILES.WP1	INDEX.HTML	OLIVER|CAT.JPG

3. Now let's review how DOS organizes files: its drive and directory structure.

- At boot, DOS assigns a drive letter to each hard drive partition and each floppy or other disk drive.

- When describing a drive, you use its letter followed by a colon. For example, hard drives start with C: and can continue to Z: if necessary. CD-ROM drives usually get the next available drive letter after the last hard drive. DOS defines these letters and will not let you change them.

- DOS names the first floppy drive A: and the second, if installed, is called B:. Again, you cannot change this. DOS cannot support more than two floppy drives because it supports the original IBM PC, which was designed for only two drives.

- Like almost every operating system, DOS uses a *hierarchical directory tree* to organize the contents of its drives. Like a tree, it starts with a single trunk (the *root directory*) and then divides into branches (*directories*), which divide into smaller branches (*subdirectories*), and so on until finally you reach the ends where you'll find the leaves (individual *files*).

✔ **Tech Note**

It helps to visualize a directory tree as upside down, because in geek-speak, the trunk, or root directory, is spoken of as if it were "above" the directories that divide it up, and those directories are spoken of as being "above" the directories into which they are divided. For example, "The file is in the Adobe directory under Program Files."

- Every file resides in some directory. Some files live in the root directory itself. Others live further down the tree.

  - Windows also uses directories, but it calls them *folders*.

  - Directories inside directories are called *subdirectories*.

  - Any directory can have multiple subdirectories.

  - Two or more files with the same name can exist in different directories on a PC, but two files in the same directory cannot have the same name.

  - In the same way, no two subdirectories under the same directory can have the same name, but two subdirectories under different directories can have the same name.

- To describe the root directory (the directory that has no other directory above it in the directory tree), you add a backslash (\) after the colon in the drive name, as in C:\.

- To describe a particular directory under the root directory, add the name of that directory after the backslash. For example, if a PC had a directory on the C: drive called TEST, you would describe it as C:\TEST.

- You display a subdirectory by adding backslashes followed by the subdirectory name. This naming convention provides a complete description of the location and name of any file. For example, if the TEST directory has a subdirectory called SYSTEM, it displays like this:

  `C:\TEST\SYSTEM`

  If the C:\TEST\SYSTEM directory contains a file called TEST2.TXT, its location is as follows:

  `C:\TEST\SYSTEM\TEST2.TXT`

- The exact location of a file in the directory tree is called its *path*.

  The path for the file TEST2.TXT in the SYSTEM subdirectory in the TEST directory on the C: drive is as follows:

  `C:\TEST\SYSTEM`

4. For each of the following files, translate the location into a path you can type at a command prompt.

a. A file named YODA.TXT in the subdirectory LUKE in the directory USETHEFORCE on the primary floppy drive:

_____

b. A file named RAINSONG.WAV in the subdirectory ZEP in the subdirectory ROCK in the directory MUSIC on the C: drive:

_____

c. A file named WEAPON.PCX in the subdirectory BOBAFETT in the subdirectory PLAYERS in the subdirectory BASEQ2 in the directory QUAKE2 on the D: drive:

_____

d. A file named AUTOEXEC.BAT in the root directory on a standard PC with a single hard drive:

_____

e. A file named CONTRACT2A.DOC in the subdirectory CONTRACTS in the subdirectory LEGAL in the directory ACCOUNT3 on a CD-ROM on a system with one hard drive, one CD-ROM drive, and one floppy drive:

_____

Lab 9.2: DOS Directory and File Management

Objective

In this lab, you will review the commands for directory and file management in DOS. At the end of this lab, you should

- Know the commands to view, navigate, create, and delete directories in DOS
- Know the commands to copy, move, rename, and delete files in DOS

Setup

This lab requires at least one working computer running Windows 98.

Process

1. Boot (or reboot) your system and hold down the F8 key to access the Windows Startup menu (see Figure 9-1).

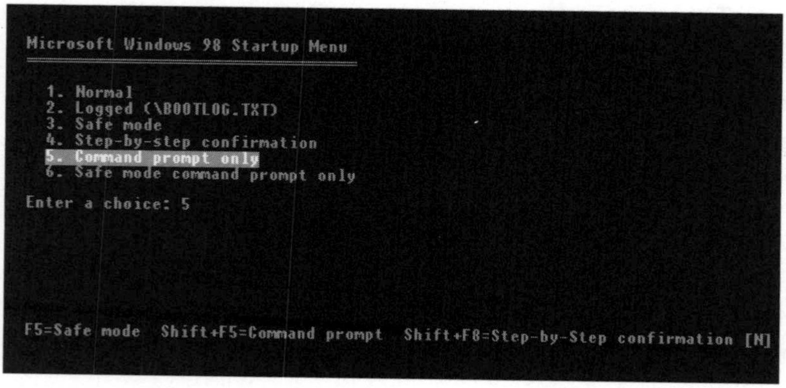

```
Microsoft Windows 98 Startup Menu

1. Normal
2. Logged (\BOOTLOG.TXT)
3. Safe mode
4. Step-by-step confirmation
5. Command prompt only
6. Safe mode command prompt only

Enter a choice: 5



F5=Safe mode   Shift+F5=Command prompt   Shift+F8=Step-by-Step confirmation [N]
```

FIGURE 9-1 Windows 98 Startup menu

2. Select Command Prompt Only and press ENTER. You should see a command prompt (C:\>).

   Probably the most frequently typed command in all of DOS is the command to display the contents of a directory (DIR). Because a command-line interface does not continually display everything the way a graphical user interface (GUI) does, you have to *ask* it if you want to know something. The way you ask DOS what is in a particular location is by focusing DOS' attention on that (sub)directory and typing **DIR**.

3. Let's see what's in your root (C:\>) directory.

   a. Type **DIR** at the command prompt and press ENTER.

→ **Note**

From now on, when you see an instruction to type a DOS command, you should assume that you are then to press ENTER. DOS will sit there waiting patiently until the sun grows cold unless you tell it to do something by pressing ENTER.

You should see something that looks like this:

```
C:\>DIR
Volume in Drive C is
Volume Serial Number is 1734-3234
Directory of C:\
DOS             <DIR>           09-03-96    9:34a
COMMAND   COM           34222   04-01-94    4:33p
AUTOEXEC  BAT           14      04-03-00    11:55a
WINDOWS         <DIR>           11-07-99    1:34a
CONFIG    SYS           34      04-03-00    4:36p
QUAKE           <DIR>           09-03-99    8:15a
YODA      DOC           55677   05-13-99    10:03a
YODA2     DOC           55832   05-13-99    10:07a
COMMAND   COM           23222   09-03-96    4:33p
9 file(s)       169001    bytes
                18288834    bytes free
```

b. Look at your particular results and note the mixture of files, which display a size in bytes (in the preceding example, YODA.DOC is 55677 bytes), and directories, which have the annotation <DIR> after the directory name (DOS, WINDOWS, and QUAKE are directories in the preceding example).

c. Note whether or not you see the following files in your root (C:\>) directory:

AUTOEXEC.BAT   Yes ____   No ____

CONFIG.SYS   Yes ____   No ____

COMMAND.COM   Yes ____   No ____

d. Write down the names of all the directories you see listed:

_____

_____

e. The biggest challenge when working with command prompts is remembering what exactly to type to achieve your goal. One assist you have is the *question mark switch*. Type **DIR /?** at the C:\> prompt and examine the options it offers you for different types of DIR listings.

f. Type **DIR /P** at the command prompt. This very useful switch causes the display to stop scrolling (pause) after each screen and waits until you press the spacebar to show you more. In directories with lots of files, this is a lifesaver!

g. Type **DIR /W** at the command prompt. This switch is convenient when you are simply looking to see if a particular file is actually in a particular directory, as it shows a "wide" list with only names, no details.

4. Now practice moving around in DOS. Right now DOS is focused on the root directory. To shift DOS' attention to (or to "point DOS at," in geek-speak) that directory, use the change directory command (CD).

a. Look at the list of directories you made and select one. Issue the CD command followed by a backslash (\) and the name of the target directory. For example, to switch to the DOS directory in the previous listing, type this:

`C:\>`**CD\DOS**

b. Do this using the directory name you selected, and then type **DIR** to see what's there. Are there any subdirectories in this directory? Make a note of them.

_____

_____

If there are no subdirectories, perform Step c and then repeat Step a using a different directory from your list. If you have a DOS or WINDOWS directory, it will almost certainly have subdirectories. Once you have found a directory with subdirectories, write them down and proceed to Step d.

c. To return to the root directory, simply type **CD** with no further information. No matter where you've gotten to, this always takes you back to the root directory. Try it now.

d. Now you'll point directly to one of the subdirectories you found. For example, if the DOS directory has a subdirectory called RULES, you should type this:

`C:\>`**CD\DOS\RULES**

Do this using the directory and subdirectory you selected, and then type **DIR** to see what's there.

e. Type **CD** followed by the name of the directory this subdirectory is in. In our example, you would type this:

`C:\DOS\RULES>`**CD\DOS**

This should take you back up to the DOS directory.

f. Now try typing a space instead of a backslash (\) between the CD command and the name of the subdirectory:

`C:\DOS>CD RULES`

You should be back in the subdirectory.

g. Typing a space only works when you are going *down* the tree one step. Try using the space to return to the directory:

`C:\DOS\RULES>CD DOS`

Oops! DOS doesn't tell you when you get it right, but it lets you know every time you do something wrong!

h. A final trick: If you want to go up a single directory level, you can type **CD** followed immediately by two periods. For example, typing this takes you up one level to the DOS directory:

`C:\DOS\RULES>CD..`

i. Take a minute and practice using the CD command. Go down a few levels on the directory tree, and then jump up a few, back to the root directory and down another path. Practice is the only way to get comfortable moving around in a command-prompt environment, and a good PC tech needs to be very comfortable doing this.

5. Now it's time to practice actually creating and deleting directories.

a. Let's create a new directory. Type **CD** to return to the root directory, where you'll add a new top-level directory. You do this using the make directory command (MD).

   1) At the command prompt, type the following:

      `C:\>MD JEDI`

   2) As usual, DOS tells you nothing—it just presents a fresh prompt. Do a DIR (that is, perform a DIR command) to see your new directory. It's as simple as that!

   3) The only caution is that DOS will create the new directory wherever it is pointing when you issue the command, whether or not that's where you meant to put it. To demonstrate, point DOS to your new directory using the CD command:

      `C:\>CD JEDI`

   4) Now use the MD command, this time creating a directory called YODA:

      `C:\JEDI>MD YODA`

5) Do a DIR again, and you should see that your JEDI directory now contains a YODA directory.

b. Return to the root directory (type **CD**) and get rid of your new directories.

1) Do this by issuing the remove directory command (RD):

```
C:\>RD JEDI
```

In a rare display of mercy, DOS responds with the following:

```
Delete directory C:\JEDI and all its subdirectories?
```

2) Press Y to eliminate both C:\JEDI and C:\JEDI\YODA.

✔ **Tech Note**

Be *very* careful when you delete things in DOS. It does not coddle you like Windows does, allowing you to change your mind and "undelete" things. When you delete a file or directory in DOS, it's gone. If you screw up, there's nothing left to do but cry. So use the computer version of the old carpenter's rule, "measure twice, cut once": DIR twice, delete once. Be sure you know *what* you're deleting before you do it and you'll save yourself a great deal of agony.

---

6. Let's turn now to managing files. DOS has some very powerful and convenient tools for this, but they can also be dangerous ones, because DOS will not question your decision to destroy hours of work with the tap of a key.

a. First, let's quickly review the use of wildcards in DOS filenames:

- *Wildcards* are two special characters, * (asterisk) and ? (question mark), that can be used in place of all or part of a filename to make a DOS command act on more than one file at a time. Wildcards work with all DOS commands that take filenames.

- The * wildcard replaces any number of letters before, or after, the dot in the filename. A good way to think of the * wildcard is "I don't care": Replace the part of the filename that you don't care about with *.

    For example, if you want to do a DIR on all the files in the root directory with the extension .EXE and you don't care what the first part of the filename is, type the following:

```
C:\>DIR *.EXE
```

This produces a directory listing of only those files with the extension .EXE— very useful when you're looking for a particular type of file. Conversely, typing **DIR YODA.*** would show you all files named YODA, regardless of their extensions. Typing **DIR Y*.*** will find all files beginning with the letter Y. And the infamous *.* (pronounced "star dot star") performs the command on all files in a directory. Useful, but very, very dangerous!

The ? wildcard replaces a single character in a filename. This can be handy when you're looking for filenames with a specific number of characters. For example, to find all files with four-character filenames and the extension .COM, type the following:

```
C:\>DIR ????.COM
```

b.   Okay, let's start playing with files! So that you can play with files safely, your first task is to create one. Boot to Windows and open Notepad (Start | Programs | Accessories | Notepad). Type **Use the Force, Luke!**, select Save As from the File menu, go to the root directory (C:), and save the file as ADVICE.TXT.

c.   Open a command prompt window either by selecting the MS-DOS Prompt item in the Start | Programs menu, or by selecting Start | Run and typing **command**. This should give you a DOS window to work in.

d.   At the C:\ prompt, type **DIR** and make sure your new file is there.

e.   Now you'll create a new directory called YODA under the root directory, so you can do some copying and moving. The only difference between copying and moving is that the original is left behind when you use COPY, but it's not left behind when you use MOVE. Once you've learned the COPY command, you've learned the MOVE command!

f.   Following are the steps for copying/moving a file.

Mike Meyers' Five-Step COPY/MOVE process:

1)   Point DOS to the directory containing the files to be copied or moved.

2)   Type **COPY** or **MOVE** and a space.

3)   Type the name of the file(s) to be copied/moved (with or without wildcards) and a space.

4)   Type the path of the new location for the files.

5)   Press ENTER.

g.   Now try it on your own. If you were successful, the root directory should contain the file ADVICE.TXT. Copy this file from the root directory to the YODA directory you just created. Follow this five-step process:

1)   If you're not pointing at the root directory, type **CD** to point DOS to C:\.

C:\NOTROOT>**CD**

2)   Type **COPY** and a space.

C:\>**COPY**

3)   Type **ADVICE.TXT** and a space.

C:\>COPY **ADVICE.TXT**

4)   Type **C:\YODA**.

C:\>COPY ADVICE.TXT **C:\YODA**

5)   Press ENTER.

The entire command and response looks like this:

C:\>COPY ADVICE.TXT C:\YODA
1 file(s) copied

h.   Do a DIR of the C: drive to see that ADVICE.TXT remains in the root directory, and then change to the YODA directory and do a DIR to see that the file was copied there.

i.   Suppose you want to save a copy of your file under a different name before you play with its contents. The COPY command does this too. Simply add the new filename to the path (as you did in Step 6), and it will make a copy under that name. For example, if you want to make a copy of ADVICE.TXT with the extension .BAK in the same directory, type the following:

C:\YODA>**COPY ADVICE.TXT ADVICE.BAK**

If you do a DIR of YODA, you will now find two copies of this file: one ending in .TXT and one ending in .BAK. As always with DOS, since you did not specify a new location, it will perform the command with reference to the current one (C:\YODA).

j.   Suppose you don't want two copies of the file, but you want to change its name because when you saved it, you goofed and gave it the wrong one. In this situation, you can use the rename command (REN). To change ADVICE.BAK to, say, USEFORCE.TXT, type the following:

C:\YODA>**REN ADVICE.BAK USEFORCE.TXT**

Notice that DOS does not confirm what it's done—it simply presents you with a fresh prompt. You must do a DIR to check your results. (Are you getting the idea that DIR is going to be your favorite DOS command?)

k. Change back to the root directory and delete the copy of ADVICE.TXT that remains there. To do this you'll use the delete command (DEL):

`C:\>DEL ADVICE.TXT`

Once again, note that not only doesn't DOS ask if you're sure you want to delete this file, it also doesn't confirm that it has done the delete. However, if you do a DIR, you'll find the file is indeed gone.

7. It's time to test yourself. Translate the following requests into DOS command syntax, and then try them out. I'm assuming that you still have the ADVICE.TXT and USEFORCE.TXT files in your C:\YODA directory and that you have DOS pointing at that directory.

a. Save a copy of ADVICE.TXT in the root directory, changing its name to YODASAYS.TXT.

b. Move YODASAYS.TXT to the YODA directory.

c. Rename all files in the YODA directory ending in .TXT to have the extension .BAK.

d. Copy USEFORCE.BAK to the root directory.

e. Rename the USEFORCE.BAK file to ADVICE.TXT.

f. Delete the YODA directory and all its contents.

g. Do a DIR of the root directory. You should see the file ADVICE.TXT, but the YODA directory should be gone.

Chapter 10

Windows 9x

Every good tech should know Windows 9x—and I don't mean from the programming side, but rather from a user's perspective. You are expected to be (eventually) the master or mistress of "All Things Tech." This might not be fair—why should a PC hardware tech know how to make a query for an Access database?—but that's the way it is. You need to be comfortable and confident with the Windows interface, or you will lose credibility as a tech. If you walk up to service a PC and have trouble moving or resizing a window, for example, this won't instill a lot of confidence in your client!

The creators of the A+ Certification exams understand this, so the exams test you on Windows user-level stuff, such as file manipulation, shifting between open applications, accessing the proper toolbar to find formatting tools, and so on. While you probably already know much of this information, these labs will help you review and perhaps catch a few bits and pieces you might have missed along the way.

Lab 10.1: Windows 9*x* Directory Structure

Objective

In this lab, you will explore the Windows 9*x* directory structure. At the end of this lab, you should

- Know how to use Windows Explorer
- Be familiar with the contents of the Windows and Program Files folders

Setup

This lab requires a working computer running Windows 98. You can do these labs on a Windows 95 machine, but some of them involve functionality only available in the 98 version.

Process

1. Let's look at the internal directory structure of Windows 9*x*.

   a. Start by opening Windows Explorer. You can find it under Programs on the Start menu.

      This program does more or less the same things as My Computer, but it looks and acts more like the old Windows 3.*x* File Manager. Besides giving you practice with another tool, Windows Explorer's handy directory tree on the left-hand side makes it much easier to see the Windows 9*x* directory structure.

      When you first look at Windows Explorer, notice that Desktop shows up right at the top of the list on the left side. Convenient, but in fact the real directory structure looks nothing like this.

   b. To see what the Windows directories really look like, first look at the C: drive (see Figure 10-1). Notice the little minus sign (-) to the left? Click it to collapse the C: drive folders.

c. Now you should see a little plus sign (+). Click it to expand the C: drive back to the way it looked when you first opened Windows Explorer.

d. All Windows 9x systems have at least two folders: Program Files and Windows. By default, applications install in Program Files. But first let's look in the Windows folder. Expand the Windows folder and look at the subdirectories.

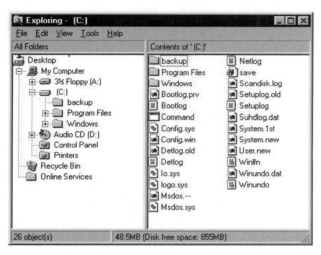

FIGURE 10-1 C:\ in Windows Explorer

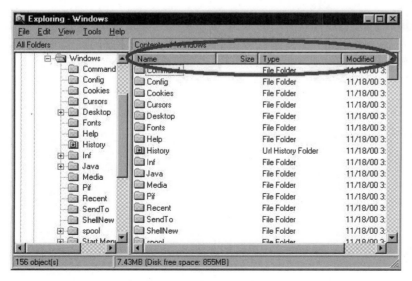

FIGURE 10-2 C:\Windows in Windows Explorer

✔ **Tech Note**

If you are using Web view, Windows 98 systems require you to click a text link called Show Files in order to see any files in the Windows folder.

e. Notice the column headers circled in Figure 10-2. Click each of these to sort by that value. Click them again to sort in reverse order. Sort by Type and see if you can locate these file types:

- INI

- BMP

- EXE

- TXT

f. Locate the SYSTEM.DAT and USER.DAT Registry files.

g. Locate WIN386.SWP, the Windows virtual memory swap file.

h. Open the WINDOWS\COMMAND subdirectory. This folder stores all the DOS-equivalent command-line programs.

1) Find FDISK.EXE and FORMAT.COM.

2) Find EDIT.COM.

i. Open the WINDOWS\COOKIES subdirectory. The cookie folder is the only place that a Web site may place data. Cookies store usernames, personalization data—anything that a Web site may want to know about you should you return to it.

✔ **Tech Note**

The cookies folder gets pretty filled on most systems and is a good place to go when you want to delete excess files, although if you do so, the next time you go to your favorite Web site you may find you have lost all your personal settings!

j. Open the WINDOWS\CURSORS subdirectory. Here's where Windows stores the many different cursors you may use.

k. Open the WINDOWS\DESKTOP subdirectory. Is this...? Yes it is! The Windows desk-top in reality is just another subfolder under Windows. If you save a file to your desktop, you're really just saving it in this folder.

You should see some of the same icons you see on your desktop. Notice that you do not see the My Computer, Recycle Bin, and Network Neighborhood icons. Microsoft has some magical way of placing those icons on the desktop. In a networking environment, users can share their desktops in order to transfer files among themselves. In order to share your desktop, you need to know the location of this folder, and now you do.

l. Open the WINDOWS\FAVORITES subdirectory. This folder stores the Web sites you save as Favorites in Internet Explorer. You can edit the contents of your Internet Explorer Favorites from this folder.

m. Open the WINDOWS\FONTS subdirectory. Like the name says, Windows stores all its fonts here. Note that fonts have one of two extensions: .FON or .TTF. FON files are old-style screen fonts. TTF files are modern TrueType fonts. Try opening a font to see what it looks like.

n. Open the WINDOWS\HELP subdirectory. This is the default location for all HLP (help) files. Open one to see what program uses it.

o. Open the WINDOWS\HISTORY subdirectory. This is the Internet Explorer History list of visited Web sites—a nice place to spy on what Web sites a person has visited! Most newer web browsers have a History option that shows you the same information from within the browser.

p. Open the WINDOWS\INF subdirectory. INF files make up the cornerstone of hardware installation.

To install any device in Windows, that device must have an INF file. The INF file tells Windows what drivers to load, what updates to place into the Registry, and what resources the device wants to use. All versions of Windows come with INF files for a broad cross-section of devices. Any new device loaded has the INF file copied here.

q. Open the WINDOWS\MEDIA subdirectory. This is the default location for sounds and audio clips. Double-click a file with a .WAV or .MID extension to hear sounds.

r. Open the WINDOWS\PIF subdirectory. Windows stores all Program Information Files (PIF) here. PIF files are used to support DOS programs.

s. Open the WINDOWS\SYSTEM subdirectory. This subdirectory is the heart of Windows 9x. Here you can see the core operating system files: GDI.EXE, KRNL386.EXE, and USER.EXE. This folder also stores almost all of the DLL files used by Windows.

Many Windows 9x systems also have a \WINDOWS\SYSTEM32 folder. This folder stores DLLs and other support files for programs designed to run under both Windows 9x and Windows NT/2000 systems.

t. Now collapse the Windows folder and expand the Program Files folder (see Figure 10-3). This is the default location for applications installed on your system. (Remember to scroll down if you can't see the end of the list.)

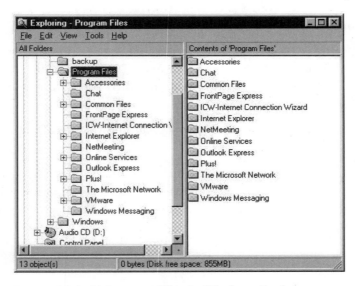

FIGURE 10-3 C:\Program Files in Windows Explorer

u. Try opening a subfolder—Accessories is a good one—and find some real programs. Look for the .EXE extension.

v. Do you see WORDPAD.EXE, or maybe MSPAINT.EXE? Double-click one to start the program. Now that you know this, you never again have to rely solely on desktop icons or the Start menu.

w. Close the program you just opened.

x. Make a list of the applications in your Program Files folder:

_____

_____

_____

y. Collapse the Program Files folder.

Lab 10.2: The Windows Desktop

Objective

In this lab, you will work with certain features of the Windows desktop. At the end of this lab, you should

- Be familiar with and comfortable using the Windows taskbar
- Be able to run programs from the Start menu
- Know how to customize the Start menu and taskbar
- Know how to change settings for the Recycle Bin

Setup

This lab requires a working computer running Windows 9x.

Process

1. The taskbar, by default, runs along the bottom of all Windows 9x desktops (although you may move it to any side: top, bottom, left, or right). The taskbar handles a number of critical jobs. Most important, it displays the Start button, probably the most frequently clicked button on all Windows systems. When you look at the taskbar, you'll notice the Start button in the far-left corner.

    a. Click the Start button.

        Clicking the Start button opens the Start menu, which is where Microsoft in its wisdom chose to put the Shut Down command. It also lists programs loaded on the system, which you can start by selecting them from the menu, and it has a Settings entry that provides access to the Control Panel and Printers applets.

b.   Move your mouse up to the Programs menu, but don't click it. As the mouse moves, notice how other menus appear.

c.   When the Programs menu appears, move your mouse to the Accessories menu.

d.   Locate the Notepad program and click it. Notepad should open in a window, and you should see a button appear on the taskbar. Most running programs show up on the taskbar in this way.

e.   Close the Notepad program by clicking the button with the "X" in the upper right-hand corner of the Notepad window. Look again at the taskbar to see that Notepad no longer appears there.

2.   Now look all the way to the right of the taskbar. This side of the taskbar is known as the *system tray*.

At the very least, you'll see the current time in the system tray, although on most Windows systems, you'll also see a number of small icons. These icons represent programs running in the background.

You often see icons in the system tray for network status, volume controls, and virus programs, and laptops may have additional icons for battery state and PC Card status. All kinds of icons show up there. What shows up in your system tray depends on your version of Windows, what hardware you use, and what programs you have loaded.

Double-click the various icons in your system tray to see what they do.

3.   Now you'll customize your environment a little.

a.   Click the Start button and choose Settings.

b.   Select Taskbar & Start Menu and click to run the applet.

c.   You should see two tabs: Taskbar Options and Start Menu Programs. Together these tabs enable you to customize many aspects of these components.

d.   Try changing the settings of each option on the Taskbar Options tab. Make a note of what each one controls.

Always on top   _____

Auto hide   _____

Show small icons in Start menu _____

Show clock _____

e. Now click the Start Menu Programs tab. You'll see several buttons you can use to alter the program selection that appears when you open the Start menu.

1) Use the Remove button to remove Notepad from the Start menu. Before you remove it, make a note of where the program is stored.

   _____

2) Use the Add button to put Notepad back in the Accessories menu, or if you prefer, in the main Programs menu.

3) Now click the Advanced button and discover the Start menu's secret: it's a special subfolder within your Windows folder. The Start menu entries are just shortcuts that Windows displays in a special way. I use this feature to move my frequently used programs to the "upper menu" that displays above Programs when you click the Start button—I just put the shortcuts in the top level of the Start menu folder.

4) As the tab tells you, the Clear button tells Windows to "forget" what you've been doing, which it otherwise records for your convenience in the Documents entry of the Start menu. If you share a computer with others, this can be a useful cleanup tool.

4. As you know, a file is not actually erased from your hard drive or other storage media when you delete it. Windows 9x and Windows 2000 add an even higher level of protection in the form of the Recycle Bin. When you delete a file in Windows, a copy of the file moves into the Recycle Bin. It stays there until you empty the Recycle Bin, restore the folder or file, or until the Recycle Bin grows larger than a preset amount.

a. To access the Recycle Bin settings, alternate-click the Recycle Bin icon and select Properties. The Recycle Bin's Properties settings look different depending on the version of Windows you have, but they all basically work the same way.

✔ **Tech Note**

Remember that everything in Windows has a Properties setting, which you can always access by alternate-clicking the object and selecting Properties. You may also access Properties by highlighting the object and pressing ALT-ENTER.

b.   Note that 10% is the default amount of drive space to use for the Recycle Bin. Change this to 5% and close Properties.

✔ **Tech Note**

If a hard drive starts to run low on space, the Recycle Bin is one of the first places to check.

Lab 10.3: Control Panel

Objective

In this lab, you will practice working with the Control Panel. At the end of this lab, you should

- Be familiar with some commonly used applets in the Control Panel
- Know how to make a Startup Disk

Setup

This lab requires a working computer running Windows 9x.

Process

1.   Open the Control Panel. There are two standard ways to do this:

- Click the Start button, scroll up to Settings, and select Control Panel. The Control Panel dialog box opens (see Figure 10-4).

- Double-click the My Computer icon on your desktop and then double-click the Control Panel icon.

2.   First you'll create a Startup Disk that you can use to boot your system in case of a problem.

a.   Insert a blank floppy disk labeled "Windows 98 Startup Disk" into your floppy drive.

b.   Double-click the Add/Remove Programs icon in the Control Panel.

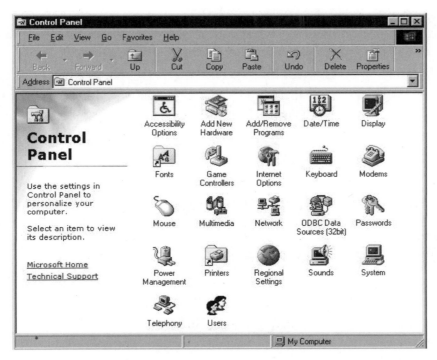

FIGURE 10-4 The Control Panel

    c.   Select the Startup Disk tab.

    d.   Click the Create Disk button.

    e.   Whether or not you have already inserted a floppy disk, you will see a dialog box instructing you to do so and warning you that the contents of that floppy will be erased when you create the startup disk. Double-check your floppy disk and then click OK.

    f.   Store your new boot disk in a place where you can find it easily in an emergency.

3.   Return to the Control Panel and double-click the Display icon.

4.   Examine each of the following Display tabs to see what it controls and experiment with making changes. Don't forget to note the current settings first.

    Background   This is where you can add wallpaper to your desktop. The default folder for these images—which must be BMP or GIF (Win98 only) files—is C:\Windows.

Screen Saver   This is where you change the screen saver settings. Note that you can preview your choice. Two important features in a corporate environment are the timer and password protection. If a screen saver has customizable features, you can click the Settings button to adjust them.

Appearance   This tab lets you change the look of your system, including the colors and fonts used to display windows and menus. It lets you save groups of settings as schemes.

Effects   This tab is where you can change your desktop icons and toggle on and off various visual effects.

Settings   This is the most "techy" of the tabs. It enables you to control the number of colors your display uses and the screen resolution (for instance, 640×480). Also, if you click the Advanced button, you can access any special features of your particular monitor/video card, including the refresh rate. Be sure you know what you're doing before you change these settings!

✔ Tech Note

If you click the Apply button after making a change instead of the OK button, the Display applet will remain open after the change takes effect—very useful when you need to experiment a bit.

5.   Close the Display applet and double-click the Keyboard icon in the Control Panel.

One thing you might not have guessed is that you can adjust your cursor's blink rate here.

Try changing the key repeat rate and delay settings. A minor adjustment here can really help a heavy-fingered user.

6.   Close the Keyboard applet and double-click the Mouse icon.

Buttons tab   This tab lets you assign actions to the different buttons (and if you have one, the scroll wheel) of the mouse.

Pointers tab   This tab lets you change the mini icons that represent your mouse pointer, such as the arrow, hourglass, and so on.

Motion tab   This tab lets you adjust the speed and tracking features of your mouse. I always adjust these settings when I install a new mouse.

7. Now that you've tweaked your mouse performance, close that applet and double-click the Sounds icon.

    a. Scroll through the Events menu and see which ones have sounds assigned to them. Are you using the Windows defaults?

    b. Select the Asterisk event. You should see the WAV file associated with this event in the Name field below.

    c. Click the little arrow button to the right of the filename to play the sound.

    d. Now click the Browse button and select a different WAV file to associate with that event.

    e. Click Apply to save your choice.

    f. Highlight the Asterisk event and play the new sound. Don't like it? Change it back.

    g. Click the drop-down menu arrow next for the Schemes field. Notice there is a Windows Default sound scheme, but if you want to alter a few sounds, you can save your new set of sounds as a separate scheme just like you could with the color and font selections in the Display applet.

8. Finally, open the Date/Time applet in the Control Panel. This applet has been around since the dawn of time, more or less, when computers didn't automatically adjust themselves for Daylight Saving Time.

    Practice adjusting the date and time. Notice you can do this either by scrolling with the arrows or by highlighting the fields. This feature can come in handy if you travel and want to change the time zone on a portable computer.

Lab 10.4: System Tools

Objective

In this lab, you will practice working with the System Tools applet. At the end of this lab, you should

- Be familiar with the tools available in the System Tools applet
- Know how to use the Disk Cleanup, System Information, ScanDisk, and Disk Defragmenter tools

Setup

This lab requires a working computer running Windows 9x.

Process

1. Click the Start button, then select Programs | Accessories | System Tools.

2. You should see the following:

   - Compression Agent
   - Disk Cleanup
   - Disk Defragmenter
   - Drive Converter
   - Drive Space
   - ScanDisk
   - Scheduled Tasks
   - System Information

3. Let's examine a few of these, starting with Disk Cleanup (see Figure 10-5).

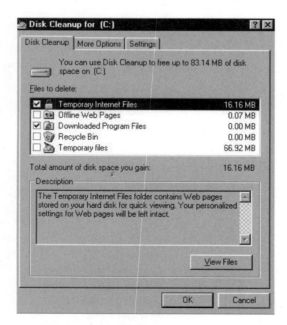

FIGURE 10-5 The Disk Cleanup utility

Starting with Windows 98, Microsoft introduced a built-in disk cleanup program called, cleverly enough, Disk Cleanup. Frankly, most third-party disk cleanup tools do a far better job, but it's not a bad little program and it does perform a very important function: it helps you get rid of the many "junk" files Windows regularly puts on your system. These junk files fall into one of six categories:

- Application temporary files that failed to delete
- Installation temporary files that failed to delete
- Internet browser cache files
- Files in the Recycle Bin
- Internet cookie files
- Identical files in separate locations

a. Open Disk Cleanup.
   How much disk space does Windows think you can clear up? _____

b. Highlight Temporary Internet Files and click the View Files button. Anything there you really need? If not, select that category and click OK to have Disk Cleanup remove the files.

4. Now open the System Information tool (see Figure 10-6). This tool is like a read-only Device Manager that shows you resource and driver information.

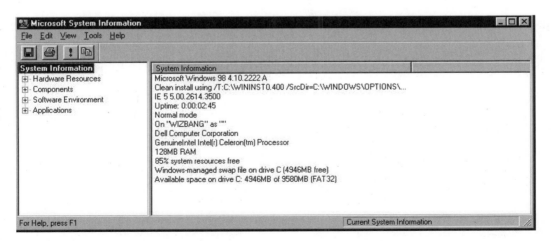

FIGURE 10-6 The System Information tool

a.   Make a note of the version of Windows you are running. _____

b.   Make a note of the amount of RAM you have. _____

c.   Make a note of the percentage of free system resources. _____

d.   Make a note of the available space on drive C:. _____

✔ **Tech Note**

If you need to run a Windows utility but you're not sure where to find it, look under the Tools menu in System Information (see Figure 10-7).

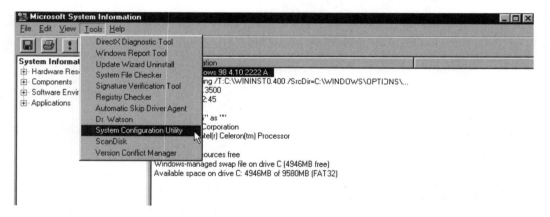

FIGURE 10-7 The Tools menu in System Information

5. Now open ScanDisk. This disk-scanning program checks for errors, just like the old Scandisk utility used to. Disk scanning is one of the two most important drive maintenance functions you can perform.

Go ahead and run the program. Any errors?

6. Finally, open the Disk Defragmenter (see Figure 10-8). Experienced PC techs still refer to it as "defrag," which was the name of the old DOS disk defragmentation utility. Although the look of defrag has changed over Windows versions, it still does the same job.

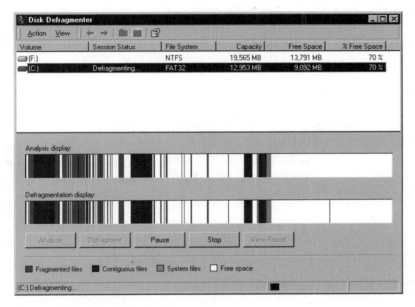

FIGURE 10-8 The Disk Defragmenter

✔ **Tech Note**

Depending on how long it's been since you last defragmented a drive and the size of the drive you're defragging, it is often advisable to start this operation when you're off to lunch or finished using your computer for the day.

If you're not in a hurry, go ahead and run Disk Defragmenter.

Lab 10.5: The Registry

Objective

In this lab, you will familiarize yourself with the Registry and REGEDIT. At the end of this lab, you should

- Know how to access the Registry using REGEDIT
- Know the functions of the six Registry Keys

Setup

This lab requires a working computer running Windows 9x.

Process

The Registry is almost never accessed directly. It is meant to work in the background, quietly storing all necessary data for the system and being updated only by the actions of a few menus and installation programs. Unfortunately, the reality is that a technician will need to manipulate the Registry from time to time. When you want to access the Registry directly, you must use the Registry Editor (REGEDIT). Remember that the Registry is a binary file. You cannot edit it with EDIT, Notepad, or any other text editor as you can with SYSTEM.INI.

1. To start the Registry Editor (shown in Figure 10-9), click the Start button, select Run, and type **REGEDIT**.

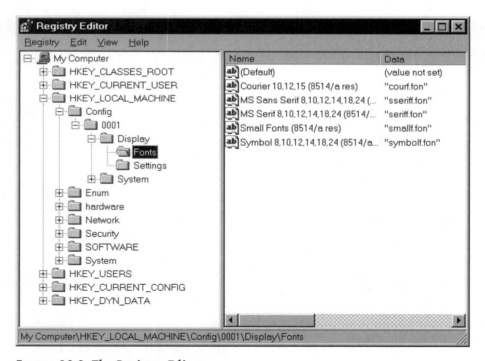

FIGURE 10-9 The Registry Editor

2. Once you open REGEDIT, you'll see six main subgroups or root keys. You should know the function of each. Try to match each root key with its function:

HKEY_CLASSES_ROOT	This key stores all of the personalization information for all users on a PC.
HKEY_CURRENT_USER	This is Registry data stored in RAM to speed up system configuration. A snapshot of all hardware in use is stored here. It is updated at boot and when any changes are made in the system configuration file.
HKEY_LOCAL_MACHINE	This key stores the current user settings, such as fonts, icons, and colors, on systems that are set up to support multiple users.
HKEY_USERS	If there are values in HKEY_LOCAL_MACHINE that have more than one option, such as two different monitors, this key defines which one is currently being used.
HKEY_CURRENT_CONFIG	This key defines the standard class objects used by Windows 9x. A *class object* is a named group of functions.
HKEY_DYN_DATA	This contains all the data for a system's non-user-specific configurations. This includes every device in your PC, including devices that you have removed.

3. Open the HKEY_CLASSES_ROOT key, and note that there are more subkeys underneath it.

   A subkey also has other subkeys and/or values.

   Notice that REGEDIT shows keys on the left and values on the right, just as Windows Explorer shows directories on the left and files on the right.

4. Okay, now we'll actually change something in the Registry. Be sure to follow the directions exactly!

   a. First, minimize all of your open windows and look at your Recycle Bin. Unless someone's been messing with your system, it should be named "Recycle Bin," but whatever it's called, write it down exactly as it appears.

   _____

b. Now close REGEDIT and then run it again (for a fresh copy). You should see My Computer highlighted at the top of the left pane.

c. Select Edit | Find to search for "Recycle Bin" (or whatever your Recycle Bin is called).

d. In the Find what field, type the exact name. Check the Match whole name only box. Only perform a Find once. There are other things with that name that you don't want to change.

e. When REGEDIT finds the file, alternate-click it and select Modify.

f. You should see the name "Recycle Bin" in the Value Data field. Try changing it to something else, like your name (or perhaps the name of someone you don't like).

g. Click OK.

h. Close REGEDIT and minimize all of your windows to see your desktop. Look the same?

i. Do a Refresh (press F5). Now you should see the name you just chose.

j. For more practice, repeat this exercise to change the name back to "Recycle Bin."

Lab 10.6: Virtual Memory

Objective

In this lab you will practice configuring your system's virtual memory. At the end of this lab, you should

- Be able to configure virtual memory using the System applet in Windows

Setup

This exercise requires a computer running Windows 9x.

Process

1. You configure virtual memory from the Performance tab in System Properties. There are two ways to get there:

- Method One

  1) Alternate-click the My Computer icon on your Desktop.

2) Select Properties.

3) Select the Performance tab.

- Method Two

    1) Open the Control Panel and double-click the System icon.

        Can you name three ways to open the Control Panel?

        _____

        _____

        _____

    2) Select the Performance tab.

2. On the Performance tab, click the Virtual Memory button.

3. Choose the Let me specify option.

    The grayed-out areas below it will now become white (available to you).

    Make a note of the amount of space available on the C: drive: _____

4. Choose a Minimum size that you would like for Virtual Memory. About 200MB should do for now. Make sure that it is less than the available hard drive space.

5. Make the Maximum size the same as the Minimum size.

6. Click the OK button. Windows will give you a warning saying that things might not work, that cats and dogs are going to start living together, whatever. Ignore the warning. You can always boot your system in Safe Mode and change things back.

7. Your system now thinks it has more RAM. Play with the settings (just don't go *too* wild!) to see what works best for you.

✔ **Tech Note**

If you have multiple drive letters on your hard drive, choose one with very little activity and use it as your virtual memory.

8. Save all of your changes, and enjoy!

Chapter 11

Windows 2000

A+ techs generally perform three essential services in a Windows 2000 environment: installation, troubleshooting, and maintenance. Techs install new systems, install hardware in existing systems, and then troubleshoot those systems when things go wrong. Techs work closely with users to maintain their systems, performing such tasks as defragmenting hard drives, running the Disk Cleanup tool, and in some environments, regularly backing up essential data. Network administrators and network technicians (such as Network+ certified techs) handle many other duties, such as running cables, adding and configuring users and groups, and so on. This lab chapter naturally focuses on the duties of A+ techs.

Techs build machines, install operating systems, configure hardware and operating systems, and fix computers when they go down. It's what we do. It's who we are. Let's do a quick rundown of the duties. Installation for A+ techs involves two basic functions: building Windows 2000 computers from the ground up, and adding and configuring new hardware in an existing Windows 2000 PC. Windows 2000 requires you to learn some new tactics and techniques to accomplish these tasks well.

Lab 11.1: Hardware Compatibility

Objective

In this lab, you will practice the first step in Windows 2000 installation: checking hardware for compatibility. At the end of this lab, you should

- Be familiar with the basic hardware requirements of Windows 2000

- Know how to check the Microsoft Hardware Compatibility List

Setup

This exercise requires Web access and a computer running Windows 9x.

Process

1. First, you must determine whether the hardware you have can actually handle Windows 2000. The minimum recommended specs for Windows 2000 are a 300+ MHz processor, 64MB of RAM, and a 2GB hard drive with about 600MB of free space. Record your machine's hardware specs here:

   _____

2. Second, you must make sure Windows 2000 will work properly with the specific components you want to install. To do this, you must access the Microsoft Hardware Compatibility List (HCL).

   a. Assemble a list of your sample PC's hardware. Write down not only the manufacturer and model, but also the chip numbers/letters you find on any expansion cards.

      _____

      _____

      _____

b. Access the Hardware Compatibility List on Microsoft's Web site (http://www.
    microsoft.com/hcl) and check for your hardware.

    If you have a Windows 2000 CD-ROM, you can also access a local copy—look in the
    SUPPORT folder on the CD-ROM for the HCL.TXT file. If possible, however, access
    the HCL on the Web, simply because it is more likely to be up-to-date.

c. Don't despair if the HCL does not contain your hardware. Many components work
    just fine under Windows 2000 without being on the HCL. In that case, however, do
    check the manufacturer's Web site to get updated drivers for the non-HCL compo-
    nents. Make a note of any non-HCL components:

    _____

Lab 11.2: Windows 2000 Installation

Objective

In this lab, you will experiment with different installations of Windows 2000. At the end of
this lab, you should

- Know how to make Windows 2000 boot disks
- Know how to install Windows 2000 onto several different hardware configurations
- Know how to convert a FAT partition to NTFS
- Know how to install an expansion card on a Windows 2000 system

Setup

This exercise requires a test machine that basically meets or exceeds Windows 2000's hardware
needs, a copy of Windows 2000 of any variety (Professional, Server, or Advanced Server), and a
couple of expansion cards that show up on the HCL. If you don't have a copy of the OS readily
available, you can get a 120-day evaluation copy of Advanced Server directly from Microsoft for
the cost of shipping. To order an evaluation copy online, visit https://microsoft.order-1.com/
Win2kEDK/default.asp. If you have a machine you can wipe or build, take the time to run
through a few different installations of Windows 2000. All five installations in this lab could
take you an entire day or longer, depending on the speed of your test machine's processor and

CD-ROM drive. (And that's assuming you don't run into too many problems.) Be prepared to spend some time on the installation. It's not particularly complex, but it can take ages.

Process

1. First make a set of boot disks. Windows 2000 does not have classic boot disks in the way that Windows 9x does. Instead, Windows 2000 has a very intelligent install/repair process. It looks for a preinstalled copy of Windows 2000, and if it detects one it shifts from an install mode into a repair mode. Most Windows 2000 systems come with four setup disks, but if you don't have them, they are simple to make. You will need four 1.44MB floppy disks.

    *   If you're running Windows 9x, use the MAKEBOOT.EXE utility on the Windows 2000 CD-ROM. You can find it in the \BOOTDISK folder.

    *   If you want to create the disks from a Windows NT/2000 system, use MAKEBT32.EXE (it's also in the \BOOTDISK folder).

✔ **Tech Note**

These setup disks are identical—you can use one set to support all Windows 2000 Professional systems.

    *   If you're really geeky, you can make a pseudo-boot floppy. Just copy these files from the root directory of your system drive onto a blank floppy disk:

    NTLDR

    NTDETECT.COM

    BOOT.INI

    NTBOOTDD.SYS (if it's there)

    Windows 2000 will boot from this pseudo-boot floppy, but it still needs a fully functional Windows 2000 boot partition. I installed Windows 2000 on my D: drive, so for me this was an easy way to boot Windows if my C: drive failed. It's also useful if any files become corrupted—even if your system and boot partition are the same. This won't be on the A+ exams, but it sure does come in handy!

2. Here are five installation variations for you to try.

a. First Installation Variation: Install the complete OS on a clean system, using all defaults.

   1) The machine should have only a basic video card, RAM, CPU, keyboard, mouse, floppy drive, CD-ROM drive, and hard drive installed.

   2) Don't use a computer that requires RAID drivers or anything fancy—just use a plain vanilla PC.

   3) Answer "Yes" to everything except networking.

b. Second Installation Variation: Install the complete OS on a clean system, but try partitioning the hard drive as FAT32, rather than NTFS.

   1) Once you have the OS installed, convert the FAT partition to an NTFS partition using the Convert utility at a command prompt.

      (a) At the command prompt, type **CONVERT [*drive:*] /FS:NTFS [/V]**.

           drive: specifies the drive to convert to NTFS.

           /FS:NTFS specifies that the volume be converted to the NTFS file system.

           /V specifies verbose mode. All messages will be displayed during conversion.

           For example, to convert the volume on drive E: from FAT to NTFS and display all messages, type **CONVERT E: /FS:NTFS /V**.

      (b) You cannot convert a drive you are currently accessing. If the Convert utility cannot lock the drive, it will offer to convert it the next time the computer restarts.

c. Third Installation Variation: Install the complete OS on a fully packed system that includes a network card.

   1) Before doing the Windows 2000 installation, see how many devices you can add on to the system. Throw everything into the mix: sound, SCSI, hopped-up video card, network card, USB controller, FireWire card, and so on.

   2) If you're a glutton for punishment or have way too much time to kill, try installing Windows 98 on the same PC. Any differences in installation?

d. Fourth Installation Variation: Create a dual-boot system by installing Windows 2000 onto a PC that is currently running Windows 9x on a FAT32 partition.

1) To create a dual-boot system you need to leave the Windows 9x OS in place, so you must install Windows 2000 in a folder that does not contain the Windows 9x files. The default locations—C:\WINDOWS for Windows 9x and C:\WINNT for Windows 2000—should work most of the time.

e. Fifth Installation Variation: Add an expansion card to a functional Windows 2000 PC.

1) Use all the normal installation procedures: unplug an ATX system, avoid ESD, have the current drivers handy, and so on.

2) Whatever card you have handy will do, even if it does not show up on the HCL. In fact, you should install a couple of cards that do not appear on the HCL just so you know what happens when Windows refuses to join in any reindeer games!

3) Once you have the card(s) installed, boot to Windows and check Device Manager. You can access Device Manager in Windows 2000 by double-clicking the System applet in the Control Panel.

A happy system will look something like Figure 11-1. If it doesn't, then it's time to move on to the next lab and read up on troubleshooting.

FIGURE 11-1 Look ma, no error marks!

Lab 11.3: Windows 2000 Troubleshooting Tools

Objective

In this lab, you will practice working with Windows 2000 troubleshooting tools. At the end of this lab, you should

- Know how to use Event Viewer
- Know how to use System Monitor
- Know how to use Device Manager

Setup

This exercise requires a working computer with Windows 2000 installed.

Process

Troubleshooting tools available in Windows 2000 include Event Viewer, System Monitor, and Device Manager, among others. You can access almost every essential tool for techs by double-clicking the Administrative Tools icon in the Control Panel and selecting Computer Management (Figure 11-2). Open the Computer Management applet.

FIGURE 11-2 The Computer Management applet

1. Look at the left-hand side of the applet window and find Event Viewer. Event Viewer shows you a running commentary of system events, including the boot process, application loads, and more. Click the plus sign (+) to expand it. You'll see at least three of the following logs: Application, Directory Service, File Replication Service, Security, and System. Record the description that appears in the right-hand pane for each:

_____

_____

_____

_____

_____

2. Click System and find an entry marked Error with a white *X* in a red circle next to it.

   Figure 11-3 shows a failed service at startup, as reported by Event Viewer.

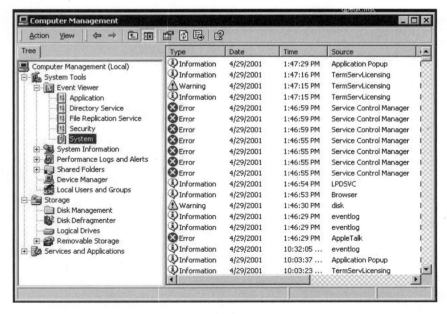

Figure 11-3 Eek! That's a lot of red and yellow!

Double-click an error listed in Event Viewer to see its details. Figure 11-4 shows the information about the logon failure shown in Figure 11-3.

FIGURE 11-4 Event Properties

3. Collapse Event Viewer and expand Device Manager. You should see a list of all your device types in the right pane. Device Manager gives you the status, including resource usage, of all your hardware. You can disable problem devices directly in Device Manager.

    a. Expand the Mice and other pointing devices entry and double-click the specific device (either one if you have two installed). You should see a Properties dialog box with two tabs: General and Driver.

    b. On the General tab, find the manufacturer and location. Record them here:

    _____

    _____

c. Click the Troubleshooting button and step through the process so you are familiar with how this application works. Since there is no actual problem, select the Skip this step option as you go through the windows.

d. Locate the Device Usage field at the bottom of the General tab and click the drop-down arrow to see the Do not use this device (disable) selection. This is how you would disable the mouse if that were necessary.

e. Now select the Driver tab. Record the mouse driver's provider, date, and version:

_____

4. You will return to the Computer Management applet in the next lab, but for now, close it and return to the Control Panel because you're going to investigate the System Monitor. One task that techs often get tagged by administrators to perform is monitoring a system that users have reported as problem-prone or buggy. Set the System Monitor to run real-time CPU- and RAM-use data as follows:

a. In the Control Panel, select Administrative Tools and open the Performance applet.

b. Highlight System Monitor on the Tree tab (see Figure 11-5).

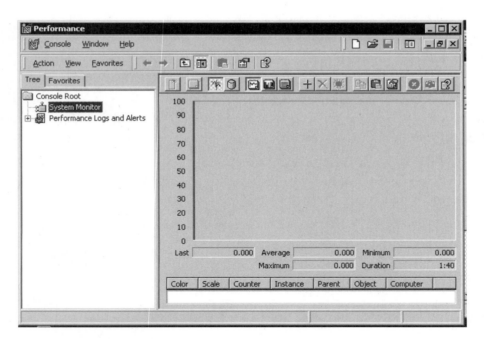

FIGURE 11-5 System Monitor

c.   Click the plus sign (+) button above the graph on the right. This will let you add counters for various Performance objects.

d.   Try adding a counter under Memory (see Figure 11-6).

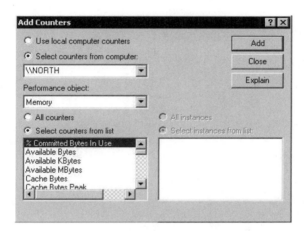

FIGURE 11-6 Memory options

e.   Now add a counter under Processor (see Figure 11-7).

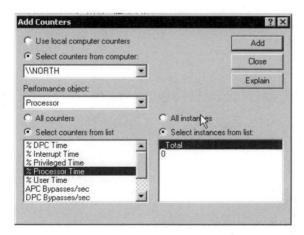

FIGURE 11-7 Processor options

f.   Watch System Monitor run while you open and close applications, surf the Web, and so on to simulate real use. Figure 11-8 shows a fairly typical display—it might be a bit hard to read in black and white, but the real one is color-coded. It should look fine on your monitor.

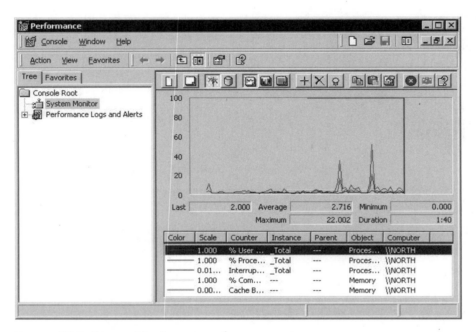

Figure 11-8 System Monitor at work

Lab 11.4: Windows 2000 Maintenance

Objective

In this lab, you will practice working with Windows 2000 maintenance tools. At the end of this lab, you should

- Know how to use Performance Logs and Alerts

- Know how to use Disk Defragmenter, ScanDisk, and Disk Cleanup

- Know how to create an Emergency Repair Disk

- Know how to create a Recovery Console

Setup

This exercise requires a working computer with Windows 2000 installed and a blank floppy disk.

Process

1. Double-click the Administrative Tools icon in the Control Panel and select Computer Management. This time expand Performance Logs and Alerts. This snap-in enables Windows 2000 to create a written record of just about anything that happens on your system. You should see three entries: Counter Logs, Trace Logs, and Alerts.

    a. Do you want to know if someone is trying to log onto your system when you're not around? Alternate-click Counter Logs and select New Log Settings. Give the new setting a name—call it anything you want. Click OK to see a screen similar to the one shown in Figure 11-9.

FIGURE 11-9 Building a new Event Log

    b. To create a new log, first click Add, and then select the Use local computer counters radio button.

c.   Next, select the Server setting from the Performance object pull-down menu.

d.   Finally, highlight Errors Logon so your dialog box looks like Figure 11-10.

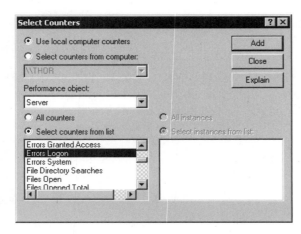

FIGURE 11-10 Good settings

e.   Select Add, and then Close.

f.   Click Schedule and set up when you want the log to run—probably from around 5 P.M. to 2 A.M.—the time period when you suspect someone might attempt to log onto your computer.

g.   Click Log Files to see the name of the file and where it's being saved—probably C:\PerfLogs (see Figure 11-11). Go back to the General tab and click OK.

h.   When you come back in the morning, open the Performance Console in Administrative Tools and select the System Monitor.

i.   Alternate-click anywhere in the graph area and select Properties.

j.   Click the Source tab and use the Browse button to locate your log file. Select the time range you want to see by dragging the small bar to the left. It should look like Figure 11-12.

k.   Now click the Data tab and select Add (see Figure 11-13). You'll only have one option—your log file—so just click Add again to see it appear.

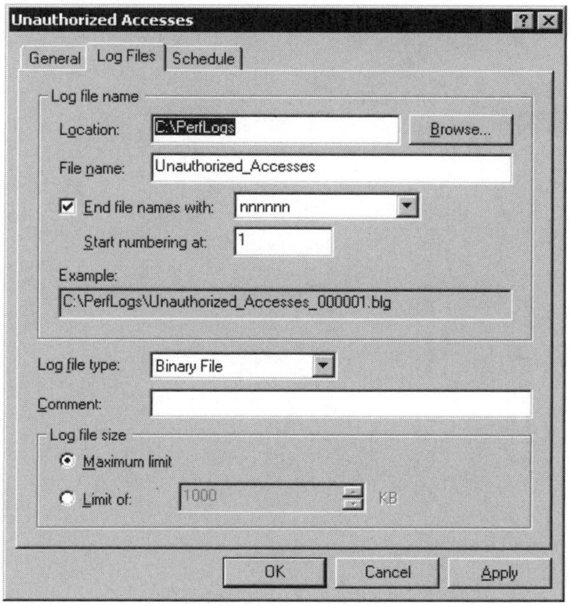

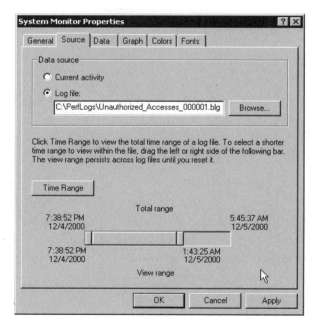

FIGURE 11-11 Log location?

FIGURE 11-12 Selecting the time range

Figure 11-13 Almost ready to go!

I. Now click OK. Do you see any bumps in the graph? Somebody has been unsuccessfully trying to log onto your system!

2. Now let's run through three tools used for an important PC tech function: routine maintenance.

   To keep your system running in an optimized condition, you should run the Disk Defragmenter on a regular basis. Access this tool by selecting the drive you wish to defragment in My Computer. Alternate-click it and select Properties. Select the Tools tab and click the Defragment Now button (see Figure 11-14).

   a. The occasional check for disk errors is also important. Access the ScanDisk tool from the Tools tab by clicking the Check Now button.

   b. As with Windows 9x, it is a good idea to run a disk cleanup periodically in Windows 2000 to remove all the junk. This tool is also in the drive Properties dialog box, on the General tab. Click the Disk Cleanup button to run this applet (see Figure 11-15).

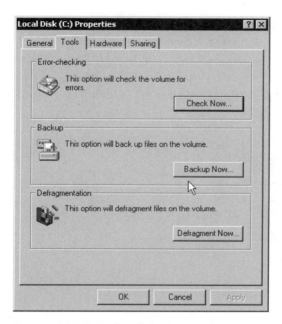

FIGURE 11-14 Tools tab in Properties

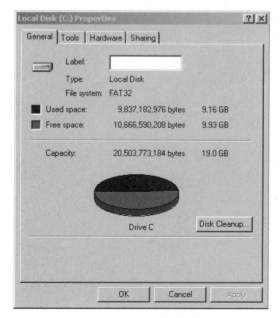

FIGURE 11-15 Disk Cleanup button

3. Just as with Windows 9x, the secret to troubleshooting Windows 2000 is preparation. Performing critical system file backups is part of this preparation. While Windows 9x really needs third-party utilities such as Hyper-Q's Q-Recovery, Windows 2000 Backup provides almost all the tools you need, although you may want to use third-party utilities to create system, e-mail, browser, and personal data backups. Open Backup from the Start menu by selecting Programs | Accessories | System Tools | Backup (see Figure 11-16).

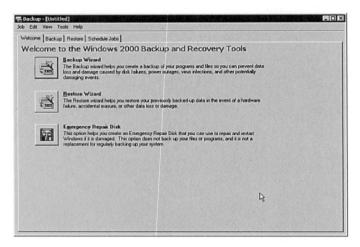

Figure 11-16 Backup

a. Let's first create an Emergency Repair Disk (ERD).

This disk saves critical boot files and partition information and is our main tool for fixing boot problems. It is not a bootable disk nor does it store very much information—the ERD does not replace a good system backup. It works with a special folder called \WINNT\REPAIR to store a copy of your registry. It's not perfect, but it gets you out of most startup problems. I always make a new ERD before I install a new device or program.

1) Click the Emergency Repair Disk button. A small pop-up window appears.

2) As instructed, insert a blank floppy disk into your floppy drive. Also select the check box, as shown in Figure 11-17, and click OK. That's it! Your ERD is now ready to save you if you need it.

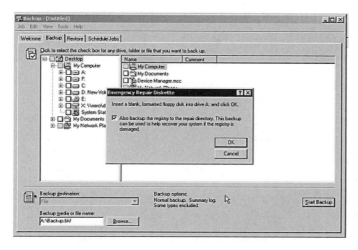

FIGURE 11-17 Creating an ERD

b. We're not quite done with Backup. Go back to the Welcome screen and click the Backup Wizard button. When the Backup wizard starts, click Next to see the screen shown in Figure 11-18.

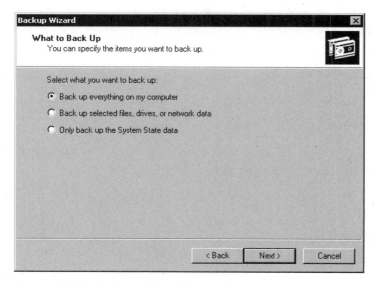

FIGURE 11-18 Backup Wizard at work

You have three options here. You are not going to run any of them right now, but you should be familiar with them. The first two are fairly self-explanatory: you can back up everything or you can just back up system-critical files.

The Only back up the System State data option enables you to save "other" system-critical files. With Windows 2000 Professional that's not much more than making an ERD with the registry backup. But the A+ Certification exams may still test you on it. Where this third option really makes sense is for Windows 2000 Server systems, because it saves Active Directory information (which your Windows 2000 Professional system does not store) as well as other critical, server-specific functions.

    c.   Close the Backup wizard without doing anything. Notice that the Backup applet is now displaying the Backup tab. Close the Backup applet as well.

4.   Now it's time to set up the unique and powerful Recovery Console—a new feature in Windows 2000. The Recovery Console is as close as Windows 2000 gets to the Windows 95/98 Safe Mode command prompt only feature.

    a.   First, you need to install it. Log onto the system with an administrator account.

    b.   Grab your Windows 2000 installation CD-ROM and drop it in your system. If the AutoPlay function kicks in, just click the No button.

    c.   Get to a Windows 2000 command prompt by typing **CMD** into the Start | Run dialog box. (CMD is the 32-bit super command prompt for Windows NT and 2000. It acts exactly like the old COMMAND.COM.)

    d.   When you get to the command prompt, switch over to the CD-ROM drive letter.

    e.   When you get to the CD-ROM drive letter, type in this command:

    \I386\WINNT32 /CMDCONS

    f.   Just follow the instructions on the screen. From now on, every time the system boots, you will see a boot menu like the one shown in Figure 11-19.

    g.   If you don't like looking at this screen, set the BOOT.INI timeout to some smaller number (but not too small!).

    h.   Reboot your system and select the Recovery Console (see Figure 11-20).

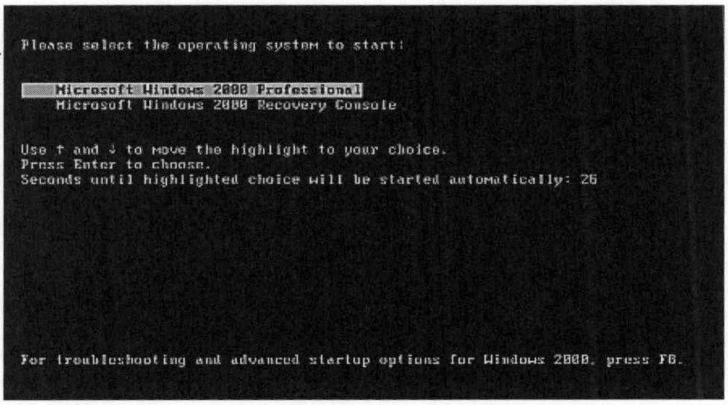

FIGURE 11-19 Boot menu after installing the Recovery Console

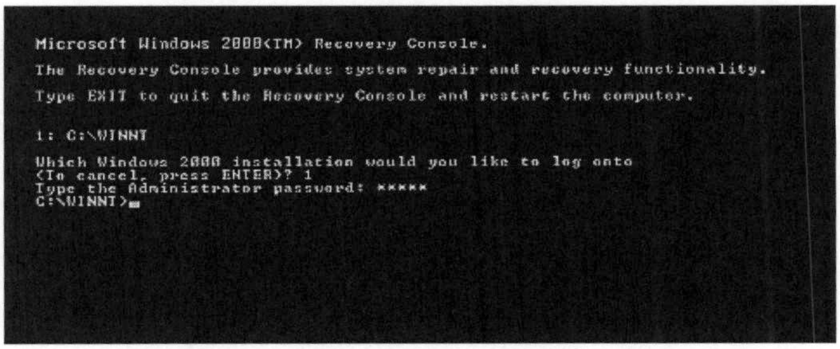

FIGURE 11-20 Recovery Console

i.   The Recovery Console looks like a command prompt (see Figure 11-20) and uses many of the commands that worked in DOS as well as some uniquely its own. Following is a list of the most common Recovery Console commands. I've added a description to some you may not have seen yet. The only ones you should try at this time are DIR, HELP, and EXIT, in that order.

ATTRIB

CD

CHKDSK

CLS: Clears the screen

COPY

DEL

DIR

DISKPART: The Windows 2000 equivalent to FDISK

EXIT: Exits the Recovery Console and restarts your computer

EXPAND

FIXBOOT: Writes a new partition table from the backup MST

FIXMBR: Equivalent to FDISK /MBR

FORMAT

HELP: Displays a Help screen

LOGON: Logs on to a Windows 2000 installation

MD

REN

RD

SYSTEMROOT: Sets the current directory to the root of the system directory, usually C:\

✔ Tech Note

The files that make up the Recovery Console reside on the system partition, making the Recovery Console useless for system partition crashes. The Recovery Console shines, however, in the business of manually restoring registries (remember where the ERD put the backup copy of the registry? You'd better remember!), rebuilding partitions (other than the system partition), or using the EXPAND program to extract copies of corrupted files from a CD-ROM or floppy disk.

Chapter 12

DOS Memory in a Windows World

If you want to make an old tech (someone who's been fixing computers for over five years) scream like a 15-year-old at a Ricky Martin concert, just sneak up behind him or her and whisper "DOS memory management." After coming down from the ceiling, the tech will get you back by droning on for hours with harrowing story after harrowing story. In the days when DOS and Windows 3.x ruled, memory management was an ongoing nightmare that tortured techs on a daily basis. The introduction of Windows 95 substantially reduced the need to understand memory management, but the installed base of DOS applications still thrives—alive and well—possibly even happily humming under the hood of your PC. So, until that final *faraway* day when we get to throw out COMMAND.COM for good, the nasty specter of DOS-based memory management still can sneak up on the unprepared PC technician. Good technicians still need to understand memory and the basic principles of memory management. In the following labs, you will review and practice some important DOS memory concepts, such as binary and hexadecimal numbers, and configuring memory allotted to DOS applications in Virtual Machines. Wow, I can sense your excitement building to a fever pitch already, so let's get started!

Lab 12.1: DOS Memory

Objective

In this lab, you will review some important DOS memory concepts. At the end of this lab, you should

- Have refreshed your knowledge of how to transpose between hexadecimal and binary numbers

- Have refreshed your knowledge of RAM addressing

Setup

This exercise requires a working brain and the calculator program that comes with Windows 9x/2000.

Process

1. Hexadecimal review

   a. What is the binary equivalent of each of the following?

   73AC6   _____

   ABCDE   _____

   12345   _____

   FFFFF   _____

   b. What is the hexadecimal equivalent of each of the following?

   10001001101010101111100   _____

   010101000011001000001   _____

   11111101111111100001   _____

   101111101110010000001   _____.

   c.   Try some of these conversions on your own using the calculator in Windows. To access the calculator, click Start | Programs | Accessories | Calculator.

       1)   From the View menu, select Scientific.

       2)   Input decimal numbers and convert them to

          •   Hexadecimal

          •   Binary

       3)   Input hexadecimal numbers and convert them to

          •   Binary

          •   Decimal

       4)   Input binary numbers and convert them to

          •   Hexadecimal

          •   Decimal

2.   Now let's see what you remember about RAM addressing.

     What is the Address range for the first megabyte of RAM? _____

     What is the classic location for the system BIOS? _____

     Where is the Reserved memory? _____

     Where is the Video RAM located?

         Graphics _____

         Mono Text _____

         Color Text   _____

     Where is the Video ROM typically located? _____

Lab 12.2: Configuring Windows Virtual Machines

Objective

In this lab, you'll put to use in a very controlled way all the steps needed to support DOS applications from within the Windows GUI. Specifically, you will change the memory configuration for the DOS-based Edit program so that it won't run, and then fix it. At the end of this lab, you should

- Have mastered the commonly used tabs and options for DOS application properties

- Have created inadequate and adequate Virtual Machines for DOS applications

Setup

This exercise requires a computer running Windows 9x.

Process

1. Using My Computer or Windows Explorer, go to the folder C:\WINDOWS\COMMAND.

2. Double-click on the file EDIT.COM to open the venerable text editor to verify that all is well, working, and otherwise hunky-dorey. When you see all is well, close the application—it's time for the fun part!

3. In C:\WINDOWS\COMMAND, alternate-click on the file EDIT.COM and select Properties from the menu to open the Edit.com Properties dialog box.

   The dialog box should have six tabs (General, Program, Font, Memory, Screen, and Misc). It opens by default with the General tab displayed, as shown in Figure 12-1. Look at Type to find where Edit is labeled an MS-DOS Application; and at Size, to find that the program weighs in at more or less 68 KB.

4. Select the Memory tab (see Figure 12-2). The top dialog area defines the amount of Conventional memory allotted to the DOS application. The Total value defines the maximum possible size for the DOS Virtual Machine in which the application will run, whereas the Initial environment value defines the starting size of the Virtual Machine.

   Note the current settings (because you'll want to return to them at the end of the exercise).

   Total _____

   Initial environment _____

   Windows' Auto settings (which the vast majority of you will just have jotted down) work amazingly well for most DOS applications, but some very persnickety applications require you to set up the memory allotment manually. Let's do it now!

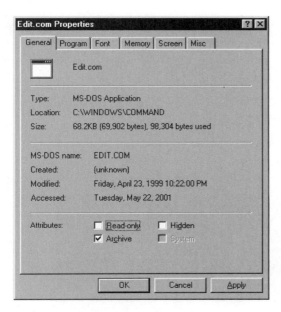

FIGURE 12-1 Edit.com Properties

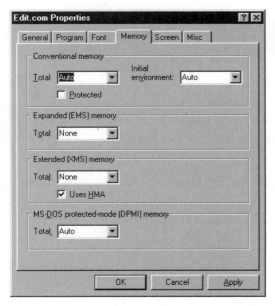

FIGURE 12-2 Edit.com default memory settings

5. Using the pull-down menu, change the amount of Total memory allotted to Edit to 40, but leave the Initial environment set to Auto. Note that the total memory this poor application is going to get is less than the size of the application itself! Think it'll work? Click the Apply button to save your changes.

6. Now double-click EDIT.COM in the C:\WINDOWS\COMMAND folder. If you followed along, you should see something similar to Figure 12-3.

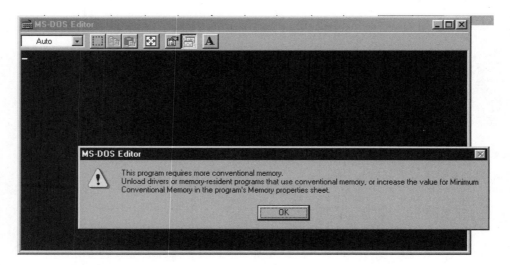

FIGURE 12-3 Oh no! I broke it!

7. Play around with the values for both the Total memory allotted and the Initial environment, selecting different combinations to see what results you get. Using these settings you can optimize the virtual machine in which a DOS application runs.

For more advanced DOS programs that require giant amounts of free conventional and expanded memory, the Memory tab in the program's executable properties is the first place to start.

Chapter 13

SCSI

In this chapter, you're going to play with some of the coolest hardware on the planet, Small Computer Systems Interface (SCSI) devices. Shugart Associates introduced SCSI in 1979 as a system-independent means of mass storage. SCSI can be best described as a "miniature network" inside your PC. Any type of peripheral can be built as a SCSI device. Common SCSI devices include hard drives, tape backup units, removable hard drives, scanners, CD-ROM drives, and printers. SCSI manifests itself through a SCSI chain, which is a series of SCSI devices working together through a host adapter. The *host adapter* is the device that attaches the SCSI chain to the PC. The key for you is to get as many different types of SCSI devices as you can find and put them together in a variety of ways. Plus, you'll want to test them in configurations that work and in configurations that do not work.

Lab 13.1: Installing SCSI Devices

Objective

In this lab, you will install and configure SCSI devices. At the end of this lab, you should

- Know how to install a SCSI host adapter

- Know how to install a SCSI hard drive

- Know how to install an external SCSI device

- Know how to create a SCSI chain

- Know how to use the SCSI configuration utility

Setup

This exercise requires a PC, cabling, and some SCSI devices. Here's an example of what I use in the classroom:

- PCI plug-and-play Adaptec 2940 (8-bit, narrow, SCSI-2) host adapter with both an internal and an external port

- SCSI hard drive with built-in terminators

- External SCSI Zip drive

- Internal SCSI CD-ROM drive that requires resistor packs installed for termination

- Any other SCSI devices I happen to have around, including other hard drives, Zip drives, and Jaz drives

- Long SCSI 50-pin ribbon cable with four or more connectors

- Active or passive 50-pin terminating resistor

- Functioning PC with Windows 98 SE/ME/2000

Process

1. Installing a SCSI device in a PC requires four basic things.

    a. First, you need to install a host adapter into a Windows PC, which means you need free resources (IRQ, I/O addresses, DMA channel, and memory addresses) and proper drivers. If you stick with a solid, well-known brand such as Adaptec, you'll have no problem at all with this step.

b. Second, you need to set termination correctly for the host adapter and any devices hooked to the host adapter.

c. Third, you need proper connectivity, including cabling and power. For some devices, you'll need drivers for Windows.

d. Finally, you need to give each device on a controller a unique SCSI ID.

e. So, to sum it up, here are the four things you need to install a SCSI device:

    • BIOS (ROM for the host adapter, drivers for devices)

    • Termination

    • Connectivity

    • ID

f. Everything assembled? Let's get to work.

2. The first thing you need to do in any SCSI installation is install the host adapter all by itself.

    Since you have a plug-and-play card, finding free resources should not be a problem. The only tricky part is dealing with the SCSI BIOS.

    Most SCSI cards have an onboard ROM chip or flash ROM chip of one sort or another (Flash, EPROM, EEPROM, and so on) that enables you to configure both the host adapter settings and the specific settings for devices you'll plug into the adapter.

    a. You'll notice the ROM loading during the boot process. Adaptec host adapters will flash a "Press <Ctrl><A> for SCSISelect<TM> Utlity!" prompt for the configuration utility (see Figure 13-1), which is precisely what you should do.

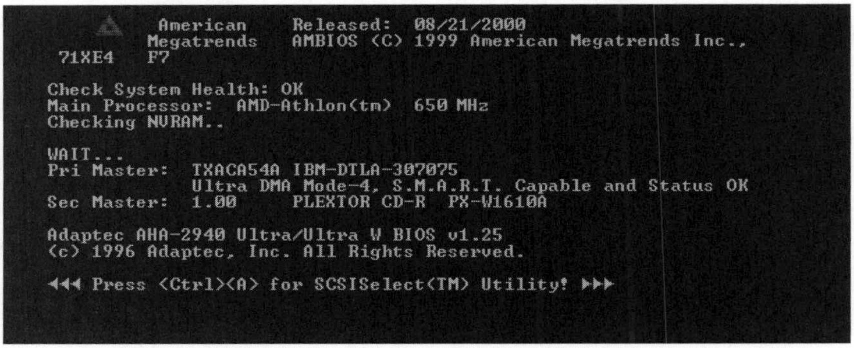

FIGURE 13-1 Adaptec host adapter prompt for configuration utility

b. When you enter the configuration utility, you have several options. Figure 13-2 displays the options for the Adaptec 2940: Configure/View Host Adapter Settings and SCSI Disk Utilities. First check the settings for the host adapter.

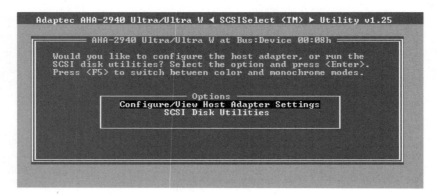

Figure 13-2 Configuration options

c. Adaptec and most other current host adapters feature an Auto setting for termination. Using Auto generally means that the host adapter senses whether it should be terminated or unterminated, depending on whether devices are plugged into one or both ports, respectively. Make sure to set your host adapter to Auto for the time being.

d. Save the configuration and reboot. This time, allow your system to boot normally and load any drivers Windows needs.

e. Check the host adapter in Device Manager. Everything cool? Let's go to the next step.

3. Most SCSI hard drives set up with no need for additional drivers, so let's do a hard drive next.

Hard drives require the same three steps as every other SCSI device: termination, cabling, and SCSI ID.

a. Set your hard drive to ID 0 and enable termination. Most hard drives have termination set internally and enable or disable by a jumper. Note the use of binary for the jumpers to set IDs, as displayed in Figure 13-3. All shunts off the ID jumpers means ID 0.

```
Adaptec AHA-2940 Ultra/Ultra W ◀ SCSISelect <TM> ▶ Utility v1.25

  ═══ AHA-2940 Ultra/Ultra W at Bus:Device 00:08h ═══
 ┌─ Configuration ──────────────────────────────────────┐
 │ SCSI Bus Interface Definitions                        │
 │   Host Adapter SCSI ID ..................... 7         │
 │   SCSI Parity Checking ..................... Enabled   │
 │   Host Adapter SCSI Termination ............ Automatic │
 │                                                       │
 │ Additional Options                                    │
 │   Boot Device Options ...................... Press <Enter> │
 │   SCSI Device Configuration ................ Press <Enter> │
 │   Advanced Configuration Options ........... Press <Enter> │
 │                                                       │
 │     <F6> - Reset to Host Adapter Defaults             │
 │                                                       │
 └───────────────────────────────────────────────────────┘
```

FIGURE 13-3 Setting the SCSI ID

b.   Once you have the hard drive set up properly, boot your system and go into the SCSI configuration utility, just as you did when you set up the host adapter. You'll find that the installation process consists of the same steps.

  1)   Install device *X* properly.

  2)   Boot and go into the SCSI configuration utility.

  3)   Find the device in the auto-scan thingy.

  4)   Save and exit.

  5)   Reboot.

  6)   Load drivers if necessary.

c.   Scan for the SCSI bus. The hard drive, if configured and connected properly, will show up on the scan with the proper ID displayed, as in Figure 13-4.

```
        ┌─ AHA-2940 Ultra/Ultra W at Bus:Device 00:08h ─┐
  Adapte│  ┌─ Select SCSI Disk and press <Enter> ─┐      │ity v1.25
        │  │ SCSI ID #0:  IOMEGA   ZIP 100         │      │
        │  │ SCSI ID #1:  No device                │      │
        │  │ SCSI ID #2:  No device                │      │
        │  │ SCSI ID #3:  No device                │      │
        │  │ SCSI ID #4:  No device                │      │
        │  │ SCSI ID #5:  No device                │      │
        │  │ SCSI ID #6:  No device                │      │
        │  │ SCSI ID #7:  AHA-2940 Ultra/Ultra W   │      │
        │  │ SCSI ID #8:  No device                │      │
        │  │ SCSI ID #9:  No device                │      │
        │  │ SCSI ID #10: No device                │      │
        │  │ SCSI ID #11: No device                │      │
        │  │ SCSI ID #12: No device                │      │
        │  │ SCSI ID #13: No device                │      │
        │  │ SCSI ID #14: No device                │      │
        │  │ SCSI ID #15: No device                │      │
        │  └───────────────────────────────────────┘      │
        └──────────────────────────────────────────────────┘
```

FIGURE 13-4 Successful scan for a SCSI hard drive

  d. Reboot your PC and allow it to go into Windows as usual.

  e. Check My Computer for your new SCSI hard drive.

4. Next, you'll add an external device.

  a. Power down your PC normally.

  b. Set the ID for the external device to something other than that of your hard drive or host adapter.

  c. Set the termination correctly for the external device.

  d. Connect everything properly.

  e. Fire up your system and go to Step 2 in the installation procedure, as outlined previously.

  f. Until you get to Windows, you should follow the same steps as for a hard drive. The main difference in Windows is you might need to load drivers.

5. Now you're ready for some SCSI-lovin' fun. Take a variety of SCSI devices, such as a CD-ROM drive, an extra hard drive, and so on, and install them one at time onto your SCSI chain.

  a. Follow the same steps that you did for the initial hard drive installation. Try the following configurations:

    • Two internal devices, one external device

    • One internal device, two external devices

    • Two or more internal devices, two or more external devices

  b. Here are some things to watch out for:

    • The major issues to watch out for with multiple devices are termination and IDs.

    • Connectivity plays an important part, of course, but if you've installed two devices successfully already, you probably have a good handle on what you should do.

    • Of course, I've never forgotten to provide power for a SCSI device. Not me. Really. I swear.

    • SCSI IDs are easy. Make certain every device has its own unique ID and you'll be fine.

6. Termination might not be as obvious as IDs. You know the rule: *Always* terminate *only* the ends of the SCSI chain.

    Terminating something in the middle or not terminating the end of a chain will cause devices to work incorrectly, right? So, the big question with multiple devices is, "Where are the 'ends' of the chain?"

    Is the host adapter always on the end? (Don't say yes, 'cause I'll have to hurt you!)

    A resounding "No!" right? If you have an internal and an external device plugged into the host adapter, the adapter's right in the *middle* of the chain.

    Should it then have termination enabled? Definitely not.

7. Look at the SCSI configurations in Figure 13-5. The image shows fairly common configurations and where to set termination.

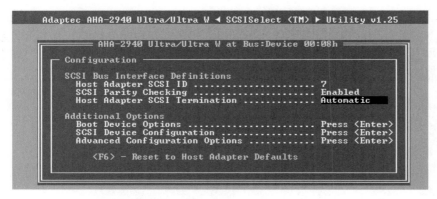

Figure 13-5 SCSI configurations and termination

Lab 13.2: Booting to SCSI

Objective

In this lab you will learn how to boot to a SCSI hard drive. At the end of this lab, you should

- Know how to boot to a SCSI hard drive

Setup

This exercise requires a working computer with a SCSI hard drive installed.

Process

1. In theory, booting to a SCSI hard drive works pretty much the same as booting to an EIDE drive. You must tell the BIOS to boot to a specific drive on a specific controller, and the drive must have a valid operating system.

2. With SCSI, you must configure two sets of BIOS: the system BIOS and the SCSI host adapter BIOS.

   a. Open CMOS to configure your system BIOS.

   b. Make certain the CMOS settings point to SCSI as the first or second boot device (after the floppy drive).

   c. If you don't have a setting on your test machine that enables you to choose either SCSI or EIDE, disable the EIDE controllers temporarily. You don't have to disconnect any drives, just disable the controllers in CMOS.

   d. Open the SCSI configuration utility.

   e. Configure the SCSI host adapter BIOS to point to the SCSI hard drive's ID as the bootable ID. You can usually find the bootable device in an Advanced option (see Figure 13-6).

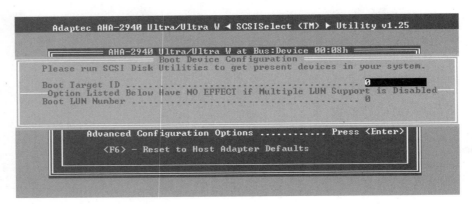

FIGURE 13-6 Bootable device ID in Adaptec host adapter

3. Save your changes and exit CMOS.

4. Allow your system to boot. If you've configured everything correctly, you should be booting to a SCSI hard drive.

Lab 13.3: Troubleshooting

Objective

In this lab you will break and fix various SCSI installations. At the end of this lab, you should

- Be able to recognize different types of problems with SCSI installations

Setup

This exercise requires a PC, cabling, and some SCSI devices, as in Lab 13.1.

Process

In this lab, you're going to purposely break and fix various SCSI installations. Trying every nondamaging "mistake" in a controlled setting enables you to recognize very quickly in the field many different types of problems.

1. Create the following errors and report the results with your combination(s) of hardware.

   a. Set the termination incorrectly.

      Take termination off one end of the chain. Does it work? _____

      What about both ends? _____

      What happens to a device on the end of a chain when you terminate something in the middle of the chain? _____

   b. To make the termination scenarios work, force your host adapter to be set as something other than Auto for termination. Set it on or off according to how you want the scenario to go.

    c.   Set the SCSI IDs incorrectly.

           What happens when two devices share an ID? _____

           What about the host adapter and a device? Does anything work?

           _____

2.   Whatever else you want to try, *do not* reverse the ribbon cables on SCSI devices. You can destroy both the device and the host adapter by doing so. This, as we say, would be a *BAD* thing.

Chapter 14
CD Media

As most folks know, the compact disc (CD) didn't begin its life in a computer. Phillips and Sony developed CDs in the late 1970s and unveiled the technology in 1980 as a replacement for vinyl records. The audio CD technology you see in music stores is still the same today as it was over 20 years ago. Audio CDs store up to 74 minutes of high-quality sound, and their high data density, random-access capability (you can jump to any spot easily), small size, and great sound make them a popular way to store music. It didn't take computer folks long to figure out that the same technology that enabled you to listen to the *Best of the Monkees* could be used to store computer data as well. CD-ROM drives soon appeared on the PC.

I like to use the term *CD media* as an umbrella term for all the nifty devices that use those shiny, 12-centimeter-wide discs that, if you're a slob like me, collect around your PCs like pizza boxes in a fraternity house. You commonly hear them called CD-ROMs (Compact Disc Read-Only Memory), but these little high-capacity beauties now cover a number of new technologies with names such as CD-R, CD-RW, and DVD.

A CD-ROM drive needs to be connected to a PC in order to operate. Since their inception, CD-ROMs in PCs have gone through a fascinating series of controllers and connections, leading to the fast, yet simple, connections we use today. ATAPI CD-ROMs have regular 40-pin IDE connectors and master/slave jumpers. You install them the same way you install any EIDE hard drive. In the following labs, you will practice removing and installing a CD-ROM drive.

Lab 14.1: Removing a CD-ROM Drive

Objective

In this lab, you will remove and inspect a CD-ROM drive. At the end of this lab, you should

- Know how to remove a CD-ROM drive safely and properly
- Be familiar with the physical features of a CD-ROM drive

Setup

This exercise requires a working computer with Windows 9x and a CD-ROM drive installed.

Process

1. Using proper ESD procedures, remove the CD-ROM drive from your system.

    a. Remove the faceplate of your PC if necessary.

    b. Remove the sides of the case.

    c. Unplug the Molex from the back of the CD-ROM.

    d. Remove the IDE cable from the CD-ROM.

    e. Unplug the audio cable from the sound card that plugs into the back of the CD-ROM.

    f.   Using a Phillips head screwdriver, remove the screws that are holding the CD-ROM in place. Notice that the screws are small threaded screws—the same type you encountered when you removed and installed your floppy drive.

    g.   Some CD-ROMs are held in their bays by rails. Simply squeeze the rail toggles to remove the CD-ROM by pulling it forward.

2.   Inspect the CD-ROM.

    a.   Look on the front of the drive for a tiny hole. You can insert a straightened-out paper clip into this hole to release the tray in case you accidentally left a CD-ROM disc in the drive prior to removing it from the system. Try inserting a straightened-out paper clip into the hole to see how it works.

    b.   You may find some or all of the following features on the front of the drive:

- A jack for headphones

- An Eject button (You should *always* close a CD-ROM by using this button. Never push the tray to close it.)

- A volume dial

- An advertisement of the drive's speed

    c.   Look at the back of the drive. You should see several areas for connections:

- The Molex-type power connection

- The connection for the flat ribbon cable. This is usually a 40-pin IDE connection. Note that the orientation or low-order pin (that is, *pin one*) is usually closest to the power connection. This could be a SCSI connection on some systems.

- Jumper settings:

  - Master

  - Slave

  - Cable select

- An audio connection to the sound card

Lab 14.2: Installing a CD-ROM Drive

Objective

In this lab you will install and configure a CD-ROM drive. At the end of this lab, you should

- Be able to install a CD-ROM drive on a Windows 9x system
- Know how to edit AUTOEXEC.BAT and CONFIG.SYS to support a CD-ROM you have installed

Setup

This exercise requires a bare-bones system (operating system and DOS files only) and a floppy disk with a CD-ROM driver and MSCDEX.EXE on it.

Process

1. Open My Computer and create a directory (folder) called CDROM in the root directory of your bootable (preferably C:) drive.

2. Copy the CD-ROM driver and the MSCDEX.EXE file from your floppy disk to the directory you just created.

3. Open a DOS window and type **EDIT CONFIG.SYS** at the prompt (make sure you spell it correctly).

    You should see a blue screen with a menu bar across the top of the screen. The cursor should be flashing in the upper left-hand corner of the blue window.

4. Type **DEVICE=C:\CDROM\[*name of the CD-ROM driver you have, including the SYS extension*]<space>D:/MSCD000** and press ENTER.

5. On the next line type **LASTDRIVE=Z** and press ENTER.

6. Hold down the ALT key and press F for file.

7. Press the x key to exit.

8. When a prompt appears that states that you have not yet saved the file, press Y to indicate that you would like to save it now.

    The file should be saved as CONFIG.SYS in the root (C:) directory.

9. Do a DIR at the prompt to see if you have a CONFIG.SYS file and check the date that it was created.

10. You're at the halfway point now. Type **EDIT AUTOEXEC.BAT** at the prompt.

(Make sure that you spell AUTOEXEC.BAT correctly!) Again, a blue window opens with a cursor in the upper left-hand corner.

11. Type **C:\CDROM\MSCDEX.EXE /D:MSCD000**.

Notice that the end of this line is exactly the same as the end of the CD-ROM driver line in CONFIG.SYS. This is the name of the device that these files are corresponding to. /D: indicates device, and MSCD000 is the name of that device.

12. Hold down the ALT key and press F for file.

13. Press the X key to exit.

14. When a prompt appears that states that you have not yet saved the file, press Y to indicate that you would like to save it now. It should be saved as AUTOEXEC.BAT in the root directory of C:.

15. Do a DIR at the prompt to see if you have an AUTOEXEC.BAT file and check the date that it was created.

16. Reboot your system and press the F8 key when you see a Starting MS-DOS or Starting Windows 9x message.

17. Do a step-by-step confirmation, and watch for the lines you just added in the CONFIG.SYS and AUTOEXEC.BAT files.

    a. Does the driver load for the CD-ROM during CONFIG.SYS? _____

    How do you know?

    _____

    b. What happens when the Lastdrive statement is run?

    _____

    c. What happens after the MSCDEX line is run in Autoexec?

    _____

    d. What is the drive letter of your CD-ROM? _____

18. Edit the AUTOEXEC.BAT file again by typing **EDIT AUTOEXEC.BAT** at a command prompt. This time when the file opens, you should see the lines that you put in there before.

19. Go to the end of the MSCDEX line, add a space, and then type **/L:R**.

The entire line should now look like this:

`C:\CDROM\MSCDEX.EXE /D:MSCD000 /L:R`

20. Hold down the ALT key and press F for file.

21. Press the x key to exit.

22. When a prompt appears that states that you have not yet saved the file, press Y to indicate that you would like to save it now.

23. Reboot your system and press the F8 key when you see a Starting MS-DOS or Starting Windows 9x message.

24. Do a step-by-step confirmation.

25. When you get to the MSCDEX line, and it is invoked

What drive letter is your CD-ROM now? _____

You should now know for sure what the function of MSCDEX is.

26. If the CD-ROM is installed—powered, cabled, and jumpered—properly, when you boot your system it should tell you if the CD-ROM is master or slave on IDE 1 or 2 (see Figure 14-1).

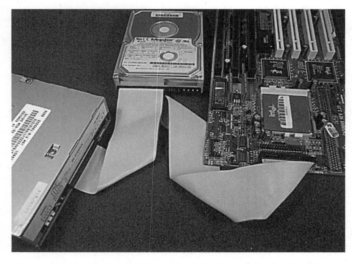

FIGURE 14-1 CD-ROM drive installed as slave with a hard drive on the primary IDE controller

Chapter 15

Sound

Basically, there are only two ways to make sounds on a PC. The first is to generate a waveform—in essence, a tape recording. A waveform can be stored digitally by taking samples at regular intervals. The quality of the recorded sound is based on how often the sound is sampled and the number of bits used for each sample. During the era of Windows 3.*x*, Microsoft adopted the WAV file format (roughly equal to CD-audio quality) for Windows. The WAV format became the de facto waveform standard, and it continues to be the most popular waveform format.

Musical Instrument Digital Interface (MIDI) is the second most popular type of sound on a PC. MIDI was not designed for the PC; it was designed to enable musicians to create, store, and play a large variety of instruments. A MIDI file functions like electronic sheet music: it contains a series of commands to play a specified note for a specified length of time on a specified instrument. The sound card follows those commands and plays the note on either emulated or recorded samples of the instrument. Because MIDI files store only these commands, they are tiny compared to WAV files. MIDI has a couple of glaring deficiencies to offset the small file size. First, MIDI files can only record instruments; you can't save a human voice or the sound of an explosion in a MIDI file. Second, MIDI playback quality depends completely on the quality of the sound card (and speakers, of course). An emulated trumpet coming from a low-end card, for example, does not sound anywhere near as nice as a sweet horn, recorded clearly and faithfully reproduced, blowing out in surround sound! The current multimedia scene has a number of technologies equated with sound, including 3-D sound, MP3 files, Dolby Digital, and DVD; but the fact remains that only two types of sound exist on a PC: waveforms and MIDI.

Waveforms and MIDI are completely different methods of creating and reproducing sounds. We need a device that can—with the help of a good device driver or two—take these two files as input and generate an analog signal to speakers or to a recording device. That device is the *sound card*. For a sound card to support both waveforms and MIDI, it must have two completely separate sets of components soldered to the card. You can think of a sound card as two devices on one card. This usually means providing separate resources (I/O addresses, IRQs, DMA channels, and drivers) for each type of sound. In these labs you'll get familiar with the resource use and installation of sound cards.

Lab 15.1: Sound Card Resources

Objective

In this lab, you will check the resources assigned to a sound card. At the end of this lab, you should

- Know how to check the resources assigned to a sound card

Setup

This exercise requires a working computer with a sound card installed.

Process

1. Open the Control Panel (you should know how to do this if you've completed the earlier labs).

2. Double-click the System icon.

3. Select the Device Manager tab.

4. Click the plus sign (+) next to Sound Devices.

5. Highlight the Sound Card icon.

6. Click the Properties button.

7. Select the Resources tab (see Figure 15-1).

FIGURE 15-1 Resource settings in Device Manager

8. Note what IRQ(s) your sound card uses: _____

9. Note the DMA channel(s):_____

10. Note the card's I/O addresses: _____

11. Exit Device Manager.

12. Close the Control Panel.

Lab 15.2: Sound Card Installation and Removal

Objective

In this lab, you will remove and reinstall a sound card. At the end of this lab, you should

 •   Know how to install and remove a sound card

Setup

This exercise requires a working computer with a sound card installed.

Process

1.   Following proper ESD procedures, remove the case from your system and find the sound card.

What type of slot is it in? _____

2.   Remove the retaining screw and carefully remove the card.

What sort of connectors does it have?   _____

Is there a volume dial on the card? _____

Does it have jumpers? _____

What is the name of the sound-processing chip? _____

Does the name of the sound-processing chip differ from the name of the manufacturer of the card? (Does the chip have "ESS" printed on it, for example, but the board has "Creative Labs" on it?) _____

Describe any cables running from the card to the CD-ROM: _____

_____

_____

Does the card have an IDE interface on it? _____

3. With the card out of your system, turn on the machine and let it boot into Windows.

4. Go to Device Manager in the Control Panel and remove the sound card.

    a. Double-click the System icon.

    b. Select the Device Manager tab.

    c. Click the plus sign (+) next to Sound Devices.

    d. Highlight the Sound Card icon.

    e. Click the Remove button.

    f. Are you sure? Yes!

5. Save your changes and shut your machine off.

6. Reboot your system, and then turn it off again. (This step is just to ensure that the card is indeed removed, and that your system recognizes the fact that it has no sound card.)

7. With the system off, replace the sound card from whence it came (as in, the same slot you pulled it from).

8. When you boot this time, your system should recognize the fact that you have added a card. Windows should prompt you that it is looking for software for the new hardware that you installed. In fact, the drivers should still be on your system.

➜ **Note**

Different versions of Windows handle the drivers differently, to say the least. You should have a current driver disk for your sound card handy just in case Windows decides that it cannot remember your sound card!

9. Open the Control Panel again.

10. Double-click the System icon.

11. Select the Device Manager tab.

12. Click the plus sign (+) next to Sound Devices.

13. Highlight the Sound Card icon.

14. Click the Properties button.

15. Select the Resources tab.

16. What IRQ is listed now? _____

17. What DMA channels are listed? _____

18. What I/O addresses are listed?_____

19. Are the settings the same as they were before you removed the card? _____

20. Make sure that your speakers are plugged into the proper jack, and test to be sure your system's sounds are audible.

21. For added amusement, go to the local computer store and check out the different sound cards available. Do they all have the same connections on the back?

Chapter 16

Video

Video consists of two devices that work as a team to get a picture in front of you: the video card, often called the *display adapter*, and the monitor. The video card has two distinct components: one to take commands from the computer and update its own onboard RAM, and the other to scan RAM and send the data to the monitor. All monitors have certain components in common, such as a cathode ray tube (CRT) and electron guns. The inside of the screen has a phosphor coating. When power is applied to one or more of the electron guns, a stream of electrons shoots toward the display end of the CRT. When the phosphor coating is struck by the electron beam, it releases its energy as visible light. Video data is displayed on the monitor as the electron guns make a series of horizontal sweeps across the display, energizing the appropriate areas of the phosphor coating. The speed at which the electron beam moves across the screen is known as the *horizontal refresh rate* (HRR). The amount of time it takes to draw the entire screen and get the electron guns back up to the upper left-hand corner is called the *vertical refresh rate* (VRR).

✖ **Warning**

Before I begin this chapter, a note of warning about the inside of a traditional monitor. Make no mistake, the interior of a monitor might look similar to the interior of a PC, with printed circuit boards and related components, but there's a big difference: no PC has voltages exceeding 15,000 to 30,000 volts, while most monitors do. So let's get one thing perfectly clear—opening up a monitor can be deadly! Even when the power is disconnected, certain components retain a substantial voltage for an extended period of time. You can inadvertently short one of the components and fry yourself—to death. Given this risk, certain aspects of monitor repair lie outside the necessary skill set for a normal PC support person, and definitely outside the A+ test domains. Make sure you understand the problems you can fix safely and the ones you need to hand over to a monitor shop.

Monitors do not determine the HRR or VRR—video cards "push" the monitor at a certain VRR and the monitor then determines the HRR. If you set a video card to push at too low a VRR, the monitor produces a noticeable flicker, causing eyestrain and headaches for users. Pushing the monitor at too high of a VRR, however, causes a definite distortion of the screen image and will damage—and eventually destroy—the circuitry of the monitor. The number one killer of monitors is improper VRR settings. All good PC support techs understand this and take substantial time tweaking the VRR to ensure that the video card pushes the monitor at the highest VRR possible without damaging the monitor—this is the Holy Grail of monitor support!

✔ **Tech Note**

When most techs say "refresh rate," they really mean the VRR.

Lab 16.1: Monitor Settings

Objective

In this lab, you will familiarize yourself with the features and settings of a monitor. At the end of this lab, you should

- Know how to change your monitor settings from the monitor itself
- Know how to check monitor settings from Windows 9x

Setup

This exercise requires a working computer with a CRT monitor running Windows 9x, and if possible, multiple monitors you can examine.

Process

1. Let's examine some monitors. If you aren't in a computer lab, try to go to your local computer store to see a wide variety.

   What sorts of external controls do they have?

   _____

   What features are present on most/all of them?

   _____

2. Play with the controls of your monitor or a test monitor. (Write down the current settings before doing any adjustments.)

   _____

   a. Change settings such as color and sizing.

   b. Put them back in their original position.

3. Now you'll practice using Windows to determine your monitor settings (without making any changes).

   a. Alternate-click your Windows 9x desktop.

    b.   Select Properties.

    c.   Go to the Settings tab. This tab displays various monitor settings, including:

        Resolution _____

        Number of colors _____

4.   The Advanced button displays more information about color settings and the display adapter. Don't make changes yet, just note the refresh rate.

        Refresh rate _____

5.   Remember to use the Cancel button to leave this area unchanged.

6.   Exit completely.

7.   Let's also take a look at any Power Management settings you may have.

    a.   Double-click the My Computer icon on your Desktop.

    b.   Go to the Control Panel and double-click the Power Management applet, if you have one.

        What sort of power management schemes do you have running?

        _____

        Note your original settings so that you can put them back if necessary.

        _____

        Make some changes to the settings and see what happens.

8.   Close the Control Panel.

Lab 16.2: Video Settings

Objective

In this lab, you will experiment with video settings. At the end of this lab, you should

- Know how to change the display settings in Windows
- Know how to change the color depth, resolution, and refresh rate

Setup

This exercise requires a working computer with a CRT monitor running Windows 9x.

✖ Warning

You are going to make changes to the look and feel of Windows. Making some of these changes can result in frustrating and time-consuming problems. Use a test machine if you have one available. If you must use your own machine, mark down all your display settings before you make any changes.

Process

1. There are several ways to navigate to the Video Properties dialog box:

    a. First navigation method

        1) Alternate-click your Windows 9x Desktop.

        2) Select Properties from the drop-down menu.

        3) Select the Settings tab.

    b. Second navigation method

        1) Click the Start button.

        2) Go to Settings.

        3) Select Control Panel.

        4) Double-click the Display icon.

        5) Select the Settings tab.

    c. Third navigation method

        1) Double-click the My Computer icon on your Desktop.

        2) Double-click the Control Panel icon.

        3) Double-click the Display icon.

        4) Select the Settings tab.

2. Before you make changes, you should first note the display settings for your PC.

   a. Alternate-click your Windows 9x Desktop.

   b. Select Properties, and then select the Settings tab. This tab displays the following monitor settings, as shown in Figure 16-1:

      • Resolution

      • Number of colors

   c. Click the Advanced button to access more information about color settings and the display adapter, including the refresh rate.

   d. Write down your display's current resolution, color depth, and refresh rate:

   _____

   e. Close that dialog box (the name usually says "*video card X* Properties"), but leave the Display Properties dialog box open.

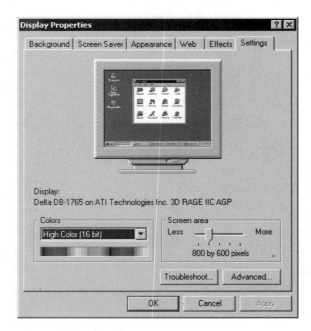

FIGURE 16-1 Display settings

3. Make some changes to the background and colors on your screen. You'll find these options on the Background and Appearance tabs. Make sure you note the original settings so you can change things back when you are done.

_____

    a. Change the background to something you might like better, such as Brick or Straw Mat.

    b. Experiment with color combinations.

→ **Note**

This is perfectly safe and easy to undo.

    c. Make some changes to the displayed fonts and menu bars.

4. Add a screensaver or change the one you currently have. You'll find these options on the Screen Saver tab. Play with the settings.

5. Check the drivers for your video card and monitor.

    a. Are they "standard" drivers or are they specific to your hardware?

    b. Can you identify the version number(s)? Write them down: _____

    c. Now get online and surf to the manufacturer's Web site.

        Check to see if there are any new drivers available.

        If new drivers are available, download and install them. (Do this on a test machine only. Get comfortable with the whole process before you do this on your personal computer.)

    d. How did this affect your machine?

6. Experiment with changing the colors and resolution of your display.

✔ **Tech Note**

Remember: If your display becomes unreadable, you can always reboot in Safe Mode to recover.

    a.   Can your machine run in 16-bit color? _____

    b.   How about 24-bit? _____

    c.   What about 800×600? _____

    d.   1024×768? _____

    e.   1280×960? _____

    f.   Any other options? _____

7.   Experiment with changing the refresh rate (see Figure 16-2).

    Can you make specific numeric changes? _____

    Are Optimal and Adapter Default the only choices you have? _____

8.   Close the Properties applet, making sure that all settings are correct.

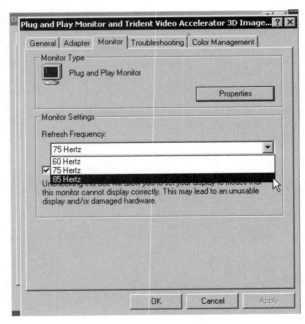

FIGURE 16-2 Typical refresh settings

Lab 16.3: The Video Card

Objective

In this lab, you will remove and examine your system's video card. At the end of this lab, you should

- Know how to remove and install a video card

- Be able to identify the make and model of a video card

- Be able to use the card information to find appropriate drivers

Setup

This exercise requires a working computer with a standard video card and a CRT monitor running Windows 9x.

→ **Note**

Certain versions of Windows have problems with changes in video cards, even one as simple as removing and reinstalling the same card. If you do this lab on a test machine, you should have no real problem if things go awry. If you use your primary PC to do the lab, however, make certain you have current drivers available for your video card or a source to get drivers if necessary.

Process

1. Let's remove the video card from your system. Remember to practice proper ESD procedures.

    a. Remove the case from your system and unplug the monitor from the card.

    b. Find the video card.

        What type of slot is your video card in? _____

    c. Remove the restraining screw and put it in a safe place.

d. Carefully but firmly remove the video card (see Figure 16-3). Be careful not to touch the expansion slot contacts on the card.

FIGURE 16-3 Video card with cooling fans

2. Examine the chips on the video card.

Do any of them give you a clue as to the card's maker? _____

Do any of them give you a clue as to the card's type? _____

Can you find the card's model? _____

Can you find the card's make? _____

Can you find the card's version? _____

3. After reading the information on the card, and knowing what type of slot it uses, do you think you could find updated drivers on the Internet? Try it. Make a note of what you find:

_____

4. Replace the video card in its slot, making sure it is seated properly.

✔ **Tech Note**

AGP cards can be a little tricky; they must be seated absolutely perfectly, or they will not work.

5. Make sure you test your system with the case still removed to see if it works. It can be frustrating and embarrassing to get the case back on, fire up the system, and get a video error. (Not that I've ever done that!)

Chapter 17

Modems

The term "modem" is the abbreviation for "modulator/demodulator." Modems are used in PCs primarily to enable computers to talk to each other through standard commercial telephone lines. Telephone wires transfer data using analog signals—that is, by continuously changing voltages on a wire. Computers hate analog signals. Computers need digital signals, voltages that are "on" or "off," meaning the wire has voltage present or it does not. Computers, being binary by nature, use only two states of voltage: zero volts and positive volts. Modems take analog signals from telephone lines and turn them into digital signals that your PC's serial ports can understand. Modems also take digital signals from the PC's serial ports and convert them into analog signals for the outgoing telephone line. This data is just a series of 1s (ones) and 0s (zeroes), which is why it's called *serial communication*. Your CPU needs to access data in discrete,

8-bit chunks, however, not in a long string of 1s and 0s. The Universal Asynchronous Receiver Transmitter (UART) chip converts the serial bits of data into 8-bit bytes that the PC can understand. All serial ports are really little more than UARTs. In these labs, you'll practice installing and configuring a modem in Windows 9x.

Lab 17.1: Modem Properties

Objective

In this lab, you will determine the properties of the modem installed on your lab machine. At the end of this lab, you should

- Know how to check the properties of an installed modem

Setup

This exercise requires a working computer running Windows 9x with a modem installed.

Process

1. Select Start | Settings | Control Panel and double-click the Modems applet.

2. Select the installed modem and click the Properties button.

   a. Can you adjust the maximum speed?_____

   b. Can you adjust the Communications Port? _____

   c. Can you adjust the port settings? _____

   d. Can you adjust the flow control?_____

3. Exit the Properties dialog box and the Control Panel, leaving your modem's properties at their original settings.

Lab 17.2: Modem Installation, Part 1

Objective

In this lab, you will use the Modems applet to install a modem. At the end of this lab, you should

- Know how to install a modem using the Modems applet in the Control Panel

Setup

This exercise requires a working computer running Windows 9x. Note that you do *not* need a modem to do this lab.

Process

Let's install a modem in a Windows 9x machine. You can do this in Windows without having an actual hardware modem.

1. Select Start | Settings | Control Panel and double-click the Modems applet.

2. Select a Standard modem of some speed (say, 28800 bps) to install.

> → **Note**
>
> Don't let Windows autodetect the modem. Select it from a list.

3. Select a port for the modem, preferably a port that your mouse is not using.

4. Select the area code that you will be dialing from.

5. If you need an outside number to initiate a call, select that.

6. Select whether you use tone or pulse dialing.

7. Click Finish.

8. Close the Modems applet and the Control Panel.

9. Now open Device Manager and remove the modem that you just installed.

Lab 17.3: Modem Installation, Part 2

Objective

In this lab, you will install a physical modem on your lab machine. At the end of this lab, you should

- Know how to install a physical modem in a PC

Setup

This exercise requires a working computer running Windows 9x and a modem to install in the machine.

Process

1. Examine the modem you're going to install.

    What type of expansion slot does it need? _____

    Do you have any of these slots open on your system?

    If you do not, you may have to remove an existing card to install the modem.

2. Using the proper ESD procedures, open your case.

3. Install the modem in the same way you installed the expansion card in Lab 5.3., remembering to use a retaining screw to hold it into place.

4. Boot to Windows. It should have autodetected the new modem (see Figure 17-1).

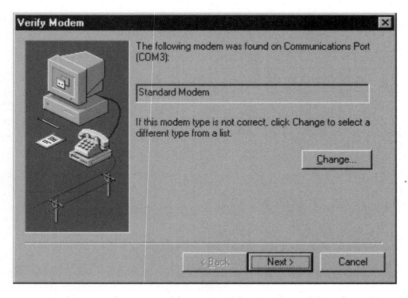

FIGURE 17-1 Windows 9x Add New Hardware wizard has found a modem

5. Do you need drivers? If so, make a note of them: _____

6. How do you set the IRQ or COM port for the modem? Make a note of the steps:

   _____

   _____

7. Check the Properties of the modem in Device Manager.

8. Make a note of the I/O and IRQ settings: _____

9. Exit Device Manager.

Chapter 18

Portable PCs

From the moment that PCs appeared in the early 1980s, people wanted to be able to move them from one location to another. The ability of a PC to hold and process data drove computer makers to come up with a way to transform the static desktop PC into a mobile device designed to serve an increasingly mobile business environment. The first generation of portable PCs were suitcase-sized "luggable" PCs, and they had some serious limitations. First, they were bulky and very heavy, some in excess of 40 pounds, so they needed a stout platform to work safely. Second, they had tiny screens due to their limited front panel area. Third, they were all AC powered—there were no batteries—so you had to be near an outlet if you wanted to compute.

It was Zenith (or possibly Data General) who first made a portable computer with a Ni-Cd battery and an LCD display, massively reducing the computer's overall size and turning a heavy, awkward, marginally mobile device into the prototypical mobile device we know today. These new mobile PCs could run anywhere thanks to their batteries and relatively low weight. In fact, the most common place for these new portables to operate was on the user's lap, and they soon became known as *laptops*. The first laptops did away with the old suitcase concept and converted mobile PCs into a shape still used today: the clamshell, keyboard-on-the-bottom, LCD-screen-at-the-top design.

Lab 18.1: Power Management

Objective

In this lab, you won't be tearing any PCs apart, but there are a few things you can do (especially with power management) that mimic the functions of portable computers. At the end of this lab, you should

- Know how to enable and disable power management in CMOS

- Know how to change power management settings in Windows

Setup

This exercise requires a working computer with Windows 9x and a BIOS that can handle power management.

Process

1. Boot your system and go into CMOS.

2. Enable power management if it is currently disabled.

3. In Windows 9x, go to the Power (Management) applet in the Control Panel.

   a. Make a note of your current power management settings:

   _____

b.   Check out the different power schemes available (this will depend on your specific system) and experiment with changing the settings.

✔ **Tech Note**

Some PCs and some components do not like standby or suspend modes. They can cause your computer to lock up. Be aware of that, and if your computer locks up, turn those settings off.

---

4.   Once you have finished experimenting, enable or disable power management as you prefer. ("Green is good," but having your hard drive shut down after one minute gets very annoying when you are trying to work.)

Lab 18.2: Field Trip!

Objective

This lab will take you into the field for a little computer browsing—for educational purposes, of course! At the end of this lab, you should

- Be familiar with the variations in key features among different portable PCs

Setup

This exercise requires a trip to a local computer store or other retailer with a good selection of portable PCs you can examine.

Process

1.   Go to your local computer or office-supply store and check out the portable PCs they have on display. Try to find a store with a variety of brands. Bring this lab manual (or a photocopy of the following chart) with you to record the different specs you find.

2. Pick out three portables, each in a different price range (to maximize differences in their features). For each portable, record the following information:

Feature	Portable #1	Portable #2	Portable #3
Size/weight	_____	_____	_____
Screen type/size	_____	_____	_____
CPU	_____	_____	_____
RAM	_____	_____	_____
Pointing device(s)	_____	_____	_____
I/O ports	_____	_____	_____
PC Card slot(s)	_____	_____	_____
Hard drive	_____	_____	_____
Floppy/CD/DVD drive(s)	_____	_____	_____

Chapter 19

Printers

Despite all of the talk about the paperless office, printers continue to be a vital part of the typical office. In many cases, PCs are used exclusively for the purpose of producing paper documents. Many people simply prefer dealing with hard copies of documents rather than electronic copies. Programmers cater to this preference by using metaphors such as "page," "workbook," and "binder" in their applications. The A+ Certification exams strongly stress the area of printing and expect a high degree of technical knowledge of the function, components, maintenance, and repair of all types of printers.

Largely obsolete in today's office environment, *impact printers* leave an image on paper by physically striking an inked ribbon against the surface of the paper. *Daisy wheel printers* (essentially an electric typewriter attached to a PC instead of directly to a keyboard) and *dot matrix printers* are the two major types of impact printers. *Inkjet printers* work by ejecting ink that has been heated to a boil by tiny resistors or electro-conductive plates through tiny tubes. They are relatively simple devices, consisting of a printhead mechanism, support electronics, a transfer mechanism to move the printhead back and forth, and a paper feed component to drag, move, and eject paper. *Laser printers* rely on the photoconductive properties of certain organic compounds. *Photoconductive* means that particles of the organic compounds, when exposed to light (that's the "photo" part), will conduct electricity. Laser printers use lasers as a light source because of their precision. Because they produce high-quality and high-speed output, laser printers have become the printers of choice in most office environments.

Lab 19.1: Parallel Modes in Windows

Objective

In this lab, we will explore the parallel port settings your computer supports. At the end of this lab, you should

- Know how to find information about parallel modes in Device Manager

- Know how to locate and change parallel port settings in CMOS

Setup

This exercise requires a working computer with Windows 9x.

Process

1. Double-click the My Computer icon on your Desktop.

2. Double-click the Control Panel icon.

3. Double-click the System applet.

4. Select the Device Manager tab.

5. Click the plus sign (+) next to Ports (COM and LPT).

    What type of port is set up next to LPT? _____

6. Do not change anything, but highlight the LPT port in the list and click Properties.

7. Select the Resources tab.

    What are the I/O and IRQs for this port?_____

8. Exit Device Manager, Control Panel, and My Computer.

9. Reboot your PC and go into CMOS.

10. Find the settings for your parallel ports. They will most likely be under a heading like Integrated Peripherals.

    a. Make a note of the settings for your parallel ports (see Figure 19-1).

    _____

    b. If you have a parallel port expansion card (this is likely on 486 and earlier machines), check the jumper settings on the card to see what options you have.

11. Experiment to see what changes you can make to the settings for the parallel ports.

12. Exit CMOS properly, without saving your changes.

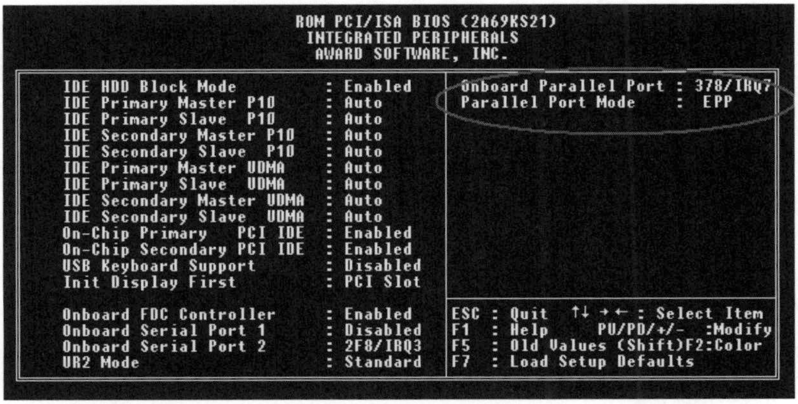

FIGURE 19-1 CMOS—Integrated Peripherals

Lab 19.2: Impact and Inkjet Printers

Objective

In this lab you will compare the features of impact and inkjet printers. At the end of this lab, you should

- Be familiar with the variations in key features between impact and inkjet printers

Setup

This exercise requires either access to impact and inkjet printers or a trip to your local computer store or other retailer with a good selection of printers you can examine.

Process

1. If you have access to an impact and an inkjet printer or two, open them up and carefully examine their insides. Also peruse the printer manual for details on their specifications.

2. If you don't have access to an impact and an inkjet printer, go to your local office supply or computer store and ask a salesperson to show you the differences between various impact and inkjet (B/W and color) printers.

3. Compare in particular the following features:

   - Speed of the printer (pages per minute)
   - Quality of the output
   - Number and types of ink cartridges
   - Price

4. What can you conclude from your comparison?

Lab 19.3: Laser Printers

Objective

In this lab you will compare the features of laser printers and practice using Windows to install a printer and change its settings. At the end of this lab, you should

- Be familiar with the variations in key features of laser printers

- Know how to install a laser printer in Windows
- Know how to change laser printer settings in Windows

Setup

This exercise requires access to a laser printer and a trip to your local computer store or other retailer with a good selection of laser printers you can examine.

Process

1. Look inside your laser printer. What parts are easily removable/replaceable?

   _____

2. Practice removing and reinserting the toner (see Figure 19-2) and paper.

✖ Warning

Remember to turn the printer off before removing anything but the toner or paper. Also, be careful not to spill any toner inside the printer.

FIGURE 19-2 Toner cartridge with its photosensitive drum exposed

3. Go to a computer or office store and have a salesperson show you the different features (and interiors) of various laser printers. Make note of the following:

How much RAM can they hold? _____

What sort of speed can they attain? _____

How does this relate to cost?_____

Are the drum and toner separate, or are they one replaceable part? _____

4. Back at your lab system, check the installed printers. Open the Printers folder in My Computer.

What properties can you set? _____

5. Now let's install a laser printer in Windows 9x. Choose Start | Settings | Control Panel and select the Printers icon.

6. Click the Add Printer icon (see Figure 19-3) and follow the steps through the Printer wizard. Add a local printer and, since the printer does not really exist, do not print a test page.

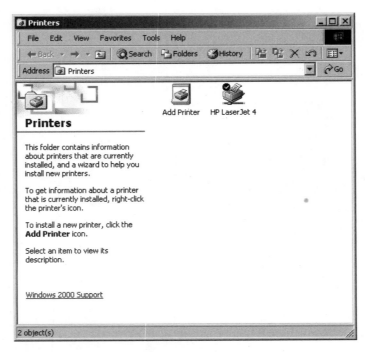

FIGURE 19-3 The Add Printer icon and the installed default printer icon

7. After you have installed the printer, reopen the Printers folder in the Control Panel, alternate-click the new printer's icon, and select Properties.

8. You should see the following options:

   - Open
   - Pause Printer
   - Set as Default
   - Purge Print Documents
   - Sharing
     - Not Shared
     - Shared as
   - Create Shortcut
   - Delete
   - Rename
   - Properties

9. Choose Start | Settings | Printers.

10. Alternate-click a laser printer icon and select Properties.

11. You should see the following options listed:

   General
   - Print Test Page

   Details
   - Print to Port
     - Add Port
     - Delete Port
   - Print Using New Driver
     - New Driver
   - Capture Printer Port/End Capture
   - Spool Settings

Sharing

- Not Shared
- Shared As
  - Share Name
  - Comment
  - Password

Paper

- Paper Size
- Orientation
  - Portrait
  - Landscape
- Media Source
- Copies

Graphics

- Resolution
- Dithering
- Intensity
- Graphics Mode
- Restore Defaults

Fonts

- Cartridges
- TrueType Fonts

Device Options

- Print Quality

✔ **Tech Note**

You should know how to find all of the previous areas.

12. Put these steps in the printing process of a laser printer in the correct order:

Charge   _____

Clean   _____

Develop   _____

Fuse   _____

Transfer   _____

Write   _____

Chapter 20

Networks

Early on in the life of the PC, it became obvious that individual PCs needed to share data and peripherals with other PCs. Certainly, any PC can read another PC's data off of floppy disks. But it takes time to copy data from one machine to a floppy, physically transport the data to another machine (a.k.a. "SneakerNet"), insert the floppy, and access the data. The process works, but it is very slow, and for certain types of data it's completely useless.

Data sharing has long been a necessity, not a luxury. Businesses need to have one database containing customer lists, product inventories, student enrollment, and so on that many users can access simultaneously. Also, businesses know they can save money if their employees share devices. Why buy everyone in the company a laser printer when a single laser printer that's accessible to everyone will suffice?

Clearly, there was a strong motivation to create a grouping of PCs—a *network*—that could enable users to share data and peripherals. Today, networking is more important than ever. Anyone working in the PC field needs to have some understanding of how it happens. The A+ Certification exams really stress knowing how to get to different network configuration screens in Windows, so I'll cover that first.

Lab 20.1: Network Configuration Options

Objective

In this lab, you will explore the Network Configuration options in Windows 9x. At the end of this lab, you should

- Know how to navigate through the Network applet

- Know where to go to share a drive

- Know where to go to specify IP addressing, gateways, or DNS addressing with TCP/IP protocols

---

➜ **Note**

Several versions of Windows 9x network properties exist and have subtle changes in the location of various tabs and options. If the following list does not precisely match your test machines, do not despair! Windows ME network properties, for example, mirror Windows 2000 layouts far more than they resemble any previous version of Windows 9x. Simply root around and you should find all of the options listed.

Setup

This exercise requires a working computer with Windows 9x.

Process

1. First let's practice navigating through the Network Configuration options.

    a.   Try these three ways to find the Network applet:

    (1)   Choose Start | Settings | Control Panel.

(2) Double-click My Computer and open the Control Panel.

(3) Alternate-click the Network Neighborhood icon on your Desktop and select Properties.

b. Double-click the Network icon to open the applet. You should see three tabs:

- Configuration

- Identification

- Access Control

c. Select the Configuration tab. You should find these components:

Add The Add button enables you to add network components. Clicking on the Add button gives you four choices:

- Client

- Adapter

- Protocol

- Service

Remove The Remove button enables you to remove network components.

Properties The Properties button displays a variety of dialog boxes based on the network component selected.

Primary Network Logon The Primary Network Logon pull-down menu can offer several options, but the most common is the *Client for Microsoft Networks* (assuming you have it installed).

File and Print Sharing Clicking on the File and Print Sharing button opens a dialog box that offers two options for sharing:

- Access to Files

- Printer Sharing

d. Select the Identification tab. You should find the following three text boxes:

- Computer Name

- Workgroup

- Computer Description

    e.   Select the Access Control tab. There's not much here to choose from. You get two radio buttons that determine how you handle passwords and control access to shared resources.

        Share-level access control   Enables you to assign different passwords for everything.

        User-level access control   Lets you use a domain server's list of users and groups so that you can specify who has access to each shared resource.

2.   Find where you set up Sharing for a particular drive.

    a.   Open My Computer and alternate-click to select the C: drive.

    b.   Choose Properties. You should see the following tabs:

- General
- Tools
- Sharing

    c.   Clearly the Sharing tab is where you want to go, so click on it. You should find about nine options (remember that options vary between different versions of Windows 9x).

        Not Shared   This radio button seems pretty self-explanatory!

        Shared As   All the other options fall under this section. You can specify the Share Name and attach a Comment to the share, for example, and set the Access Type. Windows 9x gives you three Access Types:

- Read-Only
- Full
- Depends on Password

        Each option either makes available or grays out the final two fields, which enable you to spell out the Read-Only Password and the Full Access Password text boxes.

3.   Locate the place to specify IP addressing, gateways, or DNS addressing with TCP/IP protocols.

    a.   Choose Start | Settings | Control Panel.

    b.   Double-click the Network icon.

c. Select the TCP/IP protocol (with the appropriate adapter).

d. Click the Properties button. You should see a screen similar to the one shown in Figure 20-1. Note that each tab has multiple options and that screens may differ depending on your version of Windows. You will see the following tabs:

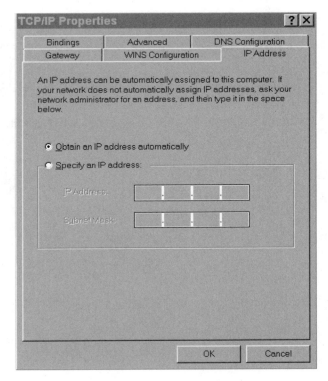

FIGURE 20-1 TCP/IP properties in a Windows 95 system

IP Address

- Obtain IP Address Automatically
- Specify IP Address

Bindings

Advanced

DNS Configuration

- Disable DNS

- Enable DNS   Clicking on this radio button brings the DNS Configuration tab to life, ungraying (what a word!) a series of options. You can add a Host, specify a Domain, and set both the DNS Server Search Order and the Domain Suffix Search Order.

Gateway   This tab enables you to add new gateways and remove installed gateways.

WINS Configuration   On the WINS Configuration tab, you can Disable WINS Resolution as an option, or Enable WINS Resolution. Choosing the latter option gives you the ability to set the WINS Server Search Order. Most systems only have the last option enabled—Use DHCP for WINS Resolution—which makes WINS irrelevant.

Lab 20.2 Networking Hardware

Objective

In this lab you will familiarize yourself with networking hardware. At the end of this lab, you should

- Be familiar with different kinds of network cabling

- Be familiar with different NICs

- Be familiar with different types of network hubs

Setup

This exercise requires access to a network, to the Web, and to a retailer selling networking hardware.

Process

1. If you have access to a network (perhaps the school's computer lab network, a friend's home network, or your company's network), spend some time exploring the hardware.

    a. What sort of cabling does it use? _____

b. What sort of NICs do the machines have? _____

c. What sort of network hubs and routers are there? _____

2. Go to your local computer store or office-supply store to check out the various networking components they have in stock. (See Figures 20-2, 20-3, and 20-4 for examples.)

a. Examine different networking cables. How can you tell them apart? _____

b. Examine different NICs. What are the key features that differentiate them? _____
_____

c. Examine different network hubs and routers. What are the key features that differentiate them? _____

3. Check out some Internet sites that sell networking hardware, such as Tiger Direct (http://www.tigerdirect.com/Category/networking.asp), and some sites that provide hardware reviews, such as CNET (http://www.cnet.com, look under Hardware Reviews: Networking).

a. Read the specifications on different NICs and network hubs.

b. Compare prices and see if you can figure out which are the best deals.

FIGURE 20-2 Thin Ethernet (802.3) 10BASE-2 cable

FIGURE 20-3 Typical rack-mounted hub

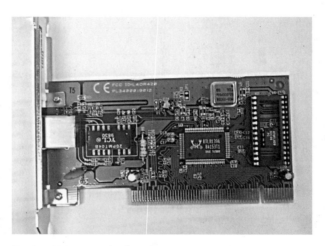

Figure 20-4 Typical NIC

Lab 20.3: Network and TCP/IP Settings

Objective

In this lab you will familiarize yourself with network and TCP/IP settings in Windows 9x, and put this knowledge into practice when you install a NIC. At the end of this lab, you should

- Be familiar with network and TCP/IP settings in Windows 9x

- Know how to install and configure a NIC

Setup

This exercise requires a computer running Windows 9x that has TCP/IP installed, File and Printer Sharing enabled, and a NIC you can install.

Process

1. Open the Network applet in the Control Panel or alternate-click Network Neighborhood and select Properties. Do not change anything—just look.

   What network card do you have, if any? _____

What protocols do you have installed? _____

Do you have File and Printer Sharing installed? _____

2. Go to your Windows 9x machine that has TCP/IP installed and File and Printer Sharing enabled.

→ **Note**

This doesn't have to be your own primary machine—it can be in a computer lab, at an Internet café, or at work.

    a.   Open the Network applet.

    b.   Highlight TCP/IP and click the Properties button.

    c.   What tabs do you see? _____

    d.   Familiarize yourself with the different tabs. Note what each one contains:

_____

_____

_____

✔ **Tech Note**

Only systems with File and Printer Sharing enabled are visible in Network Neighborhood.

3. If you are feeling very ambitious and have a spare NIC for your practice machine, go ahead and install it. You should know how to do so at this point.

    a.   Find drivers

    b.   Assign resources

    c.   Install TCP/IP

→ **Note**

You should have fun with this! Part of the learning process with PCs is to dive in and tackle a subject that you're not completely familiar with. As long as you remember your ESD procedures and write down settings before you change them, you can enjoy exploring the amazing world of computers.

Appendix A
Answer Key

Lab 1.2

5. Fill in the connector type(s) that matches each cable type.

Cable Type	Connector Type(s)
Keyboard cable	DIN, mini-DIN, or USB
Mouse cable	9-pin serial, mini-DIN, or USB
Speaker cable	Mini-audio
Monitor data cable	3-row 15-pin DB
Printer data cable (printer end)	Centronics or USB
Printer data cable (case end)	25-pin DB or USB
Network data cable	RJ-45
Modem/telephone wire	RJ-11

6. Identify the connectors pictured below. What is the name of each connector and what does it connect to?

Mini audio connectors
Speakers

15-pin (female)
Monitor

25-pin (female) DB
Printer

RJ-45
Network

15-pin (female) DB
Joystick (sound card)

36-pin Centronics
Printer

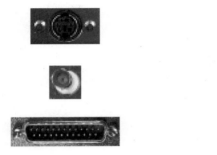

Mini-DIN
Keyboard/mouse

BNC
Network

25-pin (male) DB
Serial port (mouse)

Lab 1.3

10. Identify the components in Figure 1-6.

A 34-pin floppy drive cable

B Molex (power) connector plugged into the hard drive

C RAM sockets for 168-pin DIMMs

D DIP switches

E Cooling fan sitting atop the CPU chip

F Power supply

G AGP expansion bus slot

H PCI expansion bus slot

I ISA expansion bus slot

Lab 2.1

5. Fill in the number of data and address bus bits (wires) for each CPU in the following chart.

CPU	External Data Bus Bits	Address Bus Bits
Intel 8086	16	20
Intel 8088	8	20
Intel 80286	16	24
Intel 80386DX	32	32

CPU	External Data Bus Bits	Address Bus Bits
Intel 80386SX	<u>16</u>	<u>24</u>
AMD AM386DX	<u>32</u>	<u>32</u>
AMD AM386SX	<u>16</u>	<u>24</u>
Intel 80486DX	<u>32</u>	<u>32</u>
AMD AM486DX	<u>32</u>	<u>32</u>
Intel Pentium	<u>64</u>	<u>32</u>
AMD Athlon	<u>64</u>	<u>32</u>
AMD Duron	<u>64</u>	<u>32</u>
Intel Pentium Pro	<u>64</u>	<u>32</u>
Intel Pentium II	<u>64</u>	<u>32</u>
Intel Pentium III	<u>64</u>	<u>32</u>

6. See how many of the chip features you can fill in knowing the maker and CPU type.

	Maker	CPU Type	Package	Bus Speed (MHz)	Cache L1 (KB)	L2 (KB)	Clock Speed Multiplier
A	Intel	Pentium III 750	PPGA, FC-PGA or SECC-2	100	16T/16B	256	7.5x
B	AMD	Athlon 600	SEC	100	64T/64B	512	56x
C	AMD	Duron 800	CPGA	100	64T/64B	64	8x
D	Intel	Celeron 566	PGA	66	16T/16B	128	8.5x
E	AMD	K6-2 475	SPGA	95	32T/32B	N/A	5x
F	Intel	Pentium II 450	SEC	100	16WT/16WB	512	4.5x

7. Identify the fan types shown in Figure 2-3 (screw-down, hinged clip, or plain clip).

Fan	Type
1	<u>Hinged clip</u>
2	<u>Screw-down</u>
3	<u>Plain clip</u>

Lab 2.2

2. Identify the different socket types in Figure 2-5.

   A   <u>Socket 8</u>

   B   <u>Socket 7</u>

   C   <u>Slot 1/Slot A</u>

   D   <u>Socket 370</u>

3. Test your knowledge of chip/socket pairs. Draw a line connecting each CPU with its corresponding socket type.

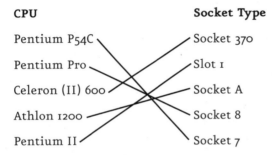

CPU	Socket Type
Pentium P54C	Socket 370
Pentium Pro	Slot 1
Celeron (II) 600	Socket A
Athlon 1200	Socket 8
Pentium II	Socket 7

Lab 3.1

4. Identify the RAM sticks in Figure 3-1 and match them with the appropriate slots in the image. Record the type and description of each and enter the matching slot number.

	Type/Description	Matching Slot #
A	<u>72-pin SIMM</u>	2
B	<u>30-pin SIMM</u>	3
C	<u>168-pin DIMM</u>	1

Lab 3.2

2. Using the preceding formula, fill in the blanks to complete the following examples.

   a. How many 30-pin SIMMs does it take to make a bank on a 386DX?

Take the width of a 30-pin SIMM (<u>8</u> bits) and divide it into the width of the EDB of a 386DX (<u>16</u> bits).

<u>16</u> ÷ <u>8</u> = <u>2</u>

It takes <u>two</u> 30-pin SIMMs to make a bank on a 386DX.

b.   How many 72-pin SIMMs does it take to make a bank on a Pentium?

Take the width of a 72-pin SIMM (<u>32</u> bits) and divide it into the width of the EDB of a Pentium (<u>64</u> bits).

<u>64</u> ÷ <u>32</u> = <u>2</u>

It takes <u>two</u> 72-pin SIMMs to make a bank on a Pentium.

c.   How many 168-pin DIMMs does it take to make a bank on a Pentium?

Take the width of a DIMM (<u>64</u> bits) and divide it into the width of the EDB of a Pentium (<u>64</u> bits).

<u>64</u> ÷ <u>64</u> = <u>1</u>

It takes <u>one</u> DIMM to make a bank on a Pentium.

d.   How many 72-pin SIMMs does it take to make a bank on a 386SX?

Take the width of the SIMM (<u>32</u> bits) and divide it into the width of the EDB of a 386SX (<u>16</u> bits).

<u>16</u> ÷ <u>32</u> = <u>0.5</u>

Therefore, it can't be done—the SIMM is wider than the EDB, and you can't break a SIMM in half and make it work.

4. Fill in the blanks to complete the following exercises.

a.   4 × 32

<u>4</u> Mb depth times <u>32</u> bits across

This tells us it is a <u>72-pin SIMM (32-bits wide)</u> and that the total volume is <u>16</u> MB.

Find out how many bytes are present by dividing <u>8</u> bits into <u>32</u> bits. The answer is <u>4</u> bytes. Then multiply that answer (<u>4</u> bytes) by the depth (<u>4</u> Mb) to get a total volume of <u>16</u> MB for a 4 × 32 SIMM.

b.   4 × 64

$\underline{4}$ Mb depth times $\underline{64}$ bits across

This tells us it is a <u>168-pin DIMM (64-bits wide)</u> and that the total volume is $\underline{32}$ MB.

Find out how many bytes are present by dividing $\underline{8}$ bits into $\underline{64}$ bits. The answer is $\underline{8}$ bytes. Then multiply that answer ($\underline{8}$ bytes) by the depth ($\underline{4}$ Mb) to get a total volume of $\underline{32}$ MB for a 4 × 64 DIMM.

6. Fill in the chart below. See how much you can do from memory.

Banking Formula	One Bank in a 386	One Bank in a 486	One Bank in a Pentium	One Bank in a Pentium II	One Bank in a Pentium III
30-pin SIMM	4	4	$\underline{8}$	$\underline{8}$	$\underline{8}$
72-pin SIMM	1	1	$\underline{2}$	$\underline{2}$	$\underline{2}$
168-pin DIMM	Won't fit!	Won't fit!	1	1	1

The relevant statistics are as follows: 386 and 486 CPUs have 32-bit external data busses; Pentium and later CPUs have 64-bit busses; 30-pin SIMMs have 8-bit data paths; 74-pin SIMMs have 32-bit data paths; and 168-pin DIMMs (and 144-pin SO-DIMMs) have 64-bit data paths.

7. Using what you learned in the preceding volume and banking exercises, try to complete the following problems.

a.   You have a Pentium system that has 128MB of RAM and two open DIMM slots. You want to add another 128MB of RAM and leave a slot available for expansion in the future. What do you need to add to your system?

   1)   Knowing that it only takes one DIMM for a bank on a Pentium, you know you will need a **X** × 64 for the system.

       Divide $\underline{8}$ bits into the $\underline{64}$ bits to get bytes for the stick. You get $\underline{8}$.

       What times $\underline{8}$ equals 128? $\underline{16}$ × $\underline{8}$ = 128.

   2)   You will need <u>one</u> <u>16</u> × <u>64</u> stick(s) to add 128MB of RAM to this system.

   3)   Do you still have an available slot? Yes

b.   You have a Pentium system with DIMMs in it equaling 160MB of RAM. You pull one stick and sell it to a friend. Your system now tallies 128MB of RAM. What did you sell your friend?

1)   Figure out the size of the stick.

160 − 128 = 32 MB

2)   X × 64 will equal 32 MB.

Divide 8 bits into 84 bits to get bytes and you get 8.

Divide 8 bytes into the 32 bytes to get 4.

3)   You sold your friend a 4 × 64.

Hope you got a decent price!

Lab 5.1

4.   Identify the expansion bus slots in Figure 5-1.

A   ISA slot

B   EISA slot

C   PCI slot

D   AGP slot

Lab 5.2

3.   List (from memory if possible) the three basic rules of I/O addresses.

All devices must have an I/O address.

All devices use more than one I/O address.

Once a device has an I/O address, no other device can use it.

4. Review Table 5-2, and then cover it up and see if you can answer the following questions.

   Which IRQs are by default open for use? <u>IRQs 2/9, 10, 11, 12</u>

   Which IRQ is by default assigned to LPT1? <u>IRQ 7</u>

   Which IRQ is by default assigned to the floppy drive? <u>IRQ 6</u>

   Which IRQ is by default assigned to the primary hard drive controller? <u>IRQ 14</u>

   Which IRQs are by default assigned to

       COM1   <u>IRQ 4</u>

       COM2   <u>IRQ 3</u>

       COM3   <u>IRQ 4</u>

       COM4   <u>IRQ 3</u>

5. a. Try writing down some binary and hex numbers at random and then try to convert them. For example:

   What is 1010 in hex? <u>A</u>

   What is 1110 1100 in hex? <u>EC</u>

   What is D3F4 in binary? <u>1101 0011 1111 0100</u>

   What is 02CB in binary? <u>0000 0010 1100 1011</u>

Lab 5.3

6. Try to identify and find the features of the expansion card in Figure 5-2.

   What type of card is it? <u>It's a video card.</u>

   What type of expansion slot does it need? <u>It needs an ISA slot.</u>

   Who is the maker of this card? <u>ATI is the maker.</u>

   How many RAM chips do you see on this card? <u>There are four RAM chips.</u>

Lab 9.1

2. Look at the following list of files. Circle those that *do not* follow the rules for 8.3 filenames:

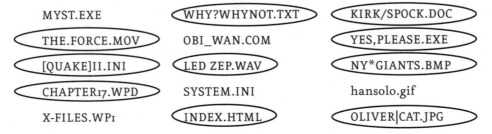

MYST.EXE   WHY?WHYNOT.TXT   KIRK/SPOCK.DOC

THE.FORCE.MOV   OBI_WAN.COM   YES,PLEASE.EXE

[QUAKE]II.INI   LED ZEP.WAV   NY*GIANTS.BMP

CHAPTER17.WPD   SYSTEM.INI   hansolo.gif

X-FILES.WP1   INDEX.HTML   OLIVER|CAT.JPG

4. For each of the following files, translate the location into a path you can type at a command prompt.

   a. A file named YODA.TXT in the subdirectory LUKE in the directory USETHEFORCE on the primary floppy drive:

   A:\USETHEFORCE\LUKE\YODA.TXT

   b. A file named RAINSONG.WAV in the subdirectory ZEP in the subdirectory ROCK in the directory MUSIC on the C: drive:

   C:\MUSIC\ROCK\ZEP\RAINSONG.WAV

   c. A file named WEAPON.PCX in the subdirectory BOBAFETT in the subdirectory PLAYERS in the subdirectory BASEQ2 in the directory QUAKE2 on the D: drive:

   D:\QUAKE2\BASEQ2\PLAYERS\BOBAFETT\WEAPON.PCX

   d. A file named AUTOEXEC.BAT in the root directory on a standard PC with a single hard drive:

   C:\AUTOEXEC.BAT

   e. A file named CONTRACT2A.DOC in the subdirectory CONTRACTS in the subdirectory LEGAL in the directory ACCOUNT3 on a CD-ROM on a system with one hard drive, one CD-ROM drive, and one floppy drive:

   D:\ACCOUNT3\LEGAL\CONTRACTS\CONTRACT2A.DOC

Lab 9.2

7. It's time to test yourself. Translate the following requests into DOS command syntax, and then try them out. I'm assuming that you still have the ADVICE.TXT and USE-FORCE.TXT files in your C:\YODA directory and that you have DOS pointing at that directory.

   a. Save a copy of ADVICE.TXT in the root directory, changing its name to YODASAYS.TXT.

      C:\YODA>COPY ADVICE.TXT C:\YODASAYS.TXT

   b. Move YODASAYS.TXT to the YODA directory.

      C:\YODA>CD..

      C:\>MOVE YODASAYS.TXT C:\YODA

   c. Rename all files in the YODA directory ending in .TXT to have the extension .BAK.

      C:\>CD YODA

      C:\YODA>REN *.TXT *.BAK

   d. Copy USEFORCE.BAK to the root directory.

      C:\YODA>COPY USEFORCE.BAK C:

   e. Rename the USEFORCE.BAK file to ADVICE.TXT.

      C:\YODA>CD..

      C:\>REN USEFORCE.BAK ADVICE.TXT

   f. Delete the YODA directory and all its contents.

      C:\>RD YODA

Lab 10.5

2. Once you open REGEDIT, you'll see six main subgroups or root keys. You should know the function of each. Try to match each root key with its function:

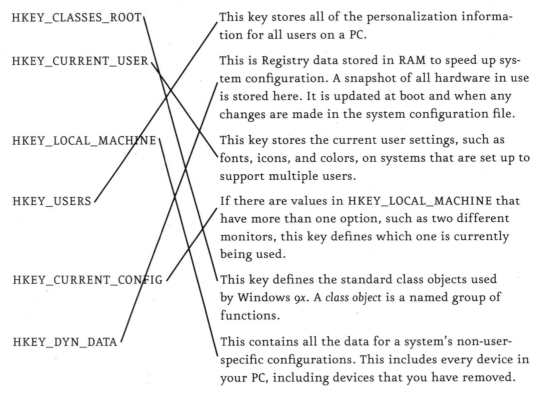

HKEY_CLASSES_ROOT — This key stores all of the personalization information for all users on a PC.

HKEY_CURRENT_USER — This is Registry data stored in RAM to speed up system configuration. A snapshot of all hardware in use is stored here. It is updated at boot and when any changes are made in the system configuration file.

HKEY_LOCAL_MACHINE — This key stores the current user settings, such as fonts, icons, and colors, on systems that are set up to support multiple users.

HKEY_USERS — If there are values in HKEY_LOCAL_MACHINE that have more than one option, such as two different monitors, this key defines which one is currently being used.

HKEY_CURRENT_CONFIG — This key defines the standard class objects used by Windows 9x. A *class object* is a named group of functions.

HKEY_DYN_DATA — This contains all the data for a system's non-user-specific configurations. This includes every device in your PC, including devices that you have removed.

Lab 10.6

1. You configure virtual memory from the Performance tab in System Properties. There are two ways to get there:

   • Method One

     1) Alternate-click the My Computer icon on your Desktop.

     2) Select Properties.

     3) Select the Performance tab.

- Method Two

  Can you name three ways to open the Control Panel?

  Start | Settings | Control Panel

  My Computer | Control Panel

  Start | Programs | Windows Explorer | Control Panel

Lab 12.1

1. Hexadecimal review

   a. What is the binary equivalent of each of the following?

   73AC6 01110011101011000110

   ABCDE 10101011110011011110

   12345 00010010001101000101

   FFFFF 11111111111111111111

   b. What is the hexadecimal equivalent of each of the following?

   10001001101010111100   89ABC

   01010100001100100001   54321

   11111101111111100001   FEFE1

   10111101110010000001   BEE41

2. Now let's see what you remember about RAM addressing.

   What is the Address range for the first megabyte of RAM? 00000-FFFFF

   What is the classic location for the system BIOS? F0000-FFFFF

   Where is the Reserved memory? A0000-FFFFF

   Where is the Video RAM located?

   Graphics A0000-AFFFF

   Mono Text B0000-B7FFF

   Color Text B8000-BFFFF

   Where is the Video ROM typically located? C0000-C7FFF

Lab 19.3

12. Put these steps in the printing process of a laser printer in the correct order:

Charge	2
Clean	I
Develop	4
Fuse	6
Transfer	5
Write	3

Index

INTERNATIONAL CONTACT INFORMATION

AUSTRALIA
McGraw-Hill Book Company Australia Pty. Ltd.
TEL +61-2-9417-9899
FAX +61-2-9417-5687
http://www.mcgraw-hill.com.au
books-it_sydney@mcgraw-hill.com

CANADA
McGraw-Hill Ryerson Ltd.
TEL +905-430-5000
FAX +905-430-5020
http://www.mcgrawhill.ca

**GREECE, MIDDLE EAST,
NORTHERN AFRICA**
McGraw-Hill Hellas
TEL +30-1-656-0990-3-4
FAX +30-1-654-5525

MEXICO (Also serving Latin America)
McGraw-Hill Interamericana Editores S.A. de C.V.
TEL +525-117-1583
FAX +525-117-1589
http://www.mcgraw-hill.com.mx
fernando_castellanos@mcgraw-hill.com

SINGAPORE (Serving Asia)
McGraw-Hill Book Company
TEL +65-863-1580
FAX +65-862-3354
http://www.mcgraw-hill.com.sg
mghasia@mcgraw-hill.com

SOUTH AFRICA
McGraw-Hill South Africa
TEL +27-11-622-7512
FAX +27-11-622-9045
robyn_swanepoel@mcgraw-hill.com

**UNITED KINGDOM & EUROPE
(Excluding Southern Europe)**
McGraw-Hill Publishing Company
TEL +44-1-628-502500
FAX +44-1-628-770224
http://www.mcgraw-hill.co.uk
computing_neurope@mcgraw-hill.com

ALL OTHER INQUIRIES Contact:
Osborne/McGraw-Hill
TEL +1-510-549-6600
FAX +1-510-883-7600
http://www.osborne.com
omg_international@mcgraw-hill.com